## NCVO PRACTICAL GUIDES

# USING THE MEDIA

Maggie Jones was born in London in 1953 and read biological sciences at Exeter University.

She has worked for a number of voluntary organisations including the Family Planning Association, where she edited *Family Planning Today*; the International Planned Parenthood Federation, as a staff writer on their quarterly development magazine, *People*, and as editor of *IPPF News*; and the National Council for Voluntary Organisations, where she was editor of the Practical Guides series.

She is now a freelance writer and author of several books, including *Trying to Have a Baby*; *Everything You Need to Know about Adoption*; *Safety and Your Child* and *Infertility: Modern Treatments and the Issues They Raise*. She has contributed to a variety of newspapers and magazines, including *The Observer*, *The Independent*, *The Guardian*, *Best* and *Parents'* magazine on health, childcare and other women's issues.

NATIONAL COUNCIL FOR VOLUNTARY ORGANISATIONS

# THE VOICE OF THE VOLUNTARY SECTOR

**Promoting the interests and effectiveness of voluntary organisations**

NCVO was established in 1919 as the representative body for charities and other organisations in England. NCVO's membership consists of some 600 members ranging from smaller self-help organisations to the biggest national charities.

NCVO has three main functions: to assist voluntary organisations through advice and information in improving their effectiveness; to promote the interests of voluntary organisations by taking part in the debate on policy issues; and to identify the need for new voluntary action in particular fields. The latter role has led NCVO to establish new organisations over the years, including Age Concern, the citizens advice bureaux network and the Charities Aid Foundation.

National Council for Voluntary Organisations
26 Bedford Square, London WC1B 3HU
Tel 071-636 4066   Fax 071-436 3188

## NCVO PUBLICATIONS
(incorporating Bedford Square Press)

NCVO publishes books on a wide range of current social issues. Series published include Survival Handbooks, Community Action, Practical Guides, Directories, Reports, Organisation and Management, and Fundraising. If you would like to receive a copy of the latest catalogue, please write to: The Sales Manager, NCVO Publications at the above address.

# Using the Media

**Maggie Jones**

Published by
NCVO Publications (incorporating Bedford Square Press)
26 Bedford Square, London WC1B 3HU

First published as *Voluntary Organisations and the Media* 1984
Second edition published as *Using the Media* 1992

Typeset in house
Printed and bound in England by J.W. Arrowsmith, Bristol
Cover printed by the Heyford Press, Wellingborough

A catalogue record for this book is available from the British Library.

ISBN   0-7199-1306-3

# Contents

# Foreword

I was delighted to be invited to write this foreword to Maggie Jones' practical guide, which introduces us to the joys and sorrows of using the media and is an excellent source of basic information.

There is no doubt that in today's world – where television and newspapers play such a prominent role in all our lives – those organisations which are prepared to take the time and trouble to develop a good working relationship with the media will benefit enormously from their efforts. This book will give those of you who are new to this field a concise step-by-step account of how this can be achieved. It also serves as an excellent reminder to those of us who are a little longer in the tooth but who have inevitably slipped into the same bad habits we advise everyone else to avoid!

Reseach is an area that must not be neglected. Complete lists of all the relevant newspapers, magazines, radio and TV companies –both local and national –are a must. So is getting to know the journalists who have an interest in your particular field and who are naturally sympathetic to your cause. Always know who you are writing to.

A press release more often than not will be your most fequent communication with the media. Newspapers and broadcasting stations are usually inundated with them.

Informing journalists of what, where, who and why, in the first paragraph of your release, is essential, particularly if it is to hold their attention long enough, and to avoid that most common of fates – the waste-paper bin. Maggie's advice in chapter 5 regarding TV and radio interviews is excellent. Anyone who has sat nerviously waiting to take part in a live interview (having of course, convinced themselves they will dry up completely) will be reminded of the importance of being well briefed.

Finally, careful planning of any media campaign, preferably well in advance, is essential, though there will of course be times when you are asked to respond immediately. Make sure there is only one point of contact for the press and that if other members of staff are required to talk to them, the same message is always given and you do not contradict someone else.

There are occasions when dealing with the media can appear intimidating but I am convinced that with the help and guidance given by Maggie Jones in this book you will soon be on your way to establishing a successful relationship of your own.

*Jane Tewson*
Director, Charity Projects and Comic Relief

# 1
# Before You Begin

When Andy Warhol made his famous statement that at some point in the not-too-distant future 'Everyone would be famous for 15 minutes', he was in fact making quite a profound statement on the nature of the media. His remark should be remembered by all voluntary organisations when it comes to seeking publicity.

Almost anything which appears in the media – press, radio, television – is quickly forgotten. News, by nature, is transient. A campaign to make people aware of the problems of, for example, disabled people, to get new volunteers, or to raise funds, may have a dramatic initial impact, but support is likely to die down again quite quickly to nearer the level that existed before. One woman, who frequently campaigned through the local media for help with her disabled son and for mothers in similar situations, said that every time people would ring up offering help in the first few days, usually more than she could deal with. They might come and help for a week or two; but then they made their excuses and she was left where she started. This is not an uncommon experience.

This said, it is true that voluntary organisations cannot exist without publicity. They need publicity for one or more of the following reasons:
- to raise money
- to recruit members
- to inform the public about the issues the voluntary organisation deals with
- to change attitudes, among the public and professional workers

- to influence government policy and legislation

Each of these aims is very different and needs a different kind of publicity. Raising money and recruiting volunteers is probably best done at a local level, unless you want and can deal with a national campaign. But if you want to put pressure on government, it's more effective to get an article in the national press, or a national radio or TV interview during peak listening or viewing times.

However, there is a danger in seeking publicity: that is, that publicity is sought for its own sake, and not because it will further the aims of an organisation. Before sending out a press release or planning a press campaign, voluntary organisations should ask themselves: what do we really want to achieve? Who do we want to respond to the publicity? Can we cope with the response generated? What if no one responds – is there a better way to get to the people we need?

Furthermore, publicity can become a drug, with people pursuing their own interests – wanting to see their name in the paper or wanting to go on the radio. The cause may become exaggerated or dramatised to get publicity, which may not help it in the long run. Publicity may also lead to unwelcome divisions within an organisation with people become jealous of the one who is in the limelight.

## What do you really want to achieve?

Deciding what you want to achieve through publicity will point you in the right direction. If your aim is to contact all local mothers of children with a particular handicap, you could achieve it by getting a number of articles in the local press, appearing on local radio, and so on. However, you may be able to get in touch with all these mothers through putting up notices in local health centres, doctors' surgeries or through other schemes aiming to help parents of handicapped children. If you use the media, you will incidentally tell a much larger audience that there are people with this kind of handicap who need help. You could use the media to help persuade these people to offer money or volunteer help. But if you do this you need to answer the question:

## Can you cope with the response generated?

Can the organisation afford to pay for the postage of letters in reply to volunteers? Will you be able to have a leaflet printed explaining your organisation's aims? Do you have people to answer the telephone and deal with all the enquiries generated? Will you be inundated with volunteers whom you don't really want and can't provide work for? What kind of impression of your organisation will this give the people who want to help?

As an example, Age Concern (England) were telephoned out of the blue by one of the popular Fleet Street papers who had suddenly decided to do an appeal for volunteers to work with elderly people. They wanted to publish the names and addresses of Age Concern branches throughout the country. Age Concern has 1100 local groups throughout England, most of whom would not have the resources to develop and operate a system to deal with a large response without at least a week's notice. It would also take several days for the central office to inform the major groups and for them to pass the message on to their own local groups.

Meanwhile, other journalists were telephoning other branches of Age Concern and also getting a hesitant response. The newspaper's editor became very angry, was unable to understand this attitude and began to think of running another article slamming agencies like Age Concern which were hedged with bureaucracy and didn't have the best interests of elderly people at heart. Age Concern's press officer fortunately got wind of this, and spoke to the editor at some length to explain the situation. She persuaded him that if he delayed the article and gave them time to warn local groups, devise a system for organising the replies to volunteers so that they would not be disappointed, and so on, this would be of the greatest benefit to old people. In the end this is what happened.

The moral of the story is that you have to put yourself in the journalists's shoes and see how he or she will interpret your response. It is no good saying you can't do it and being irritated with the press – which may result in bad publicity. Nor is it any good saying 'go ahead' without thinking through how you will deal with the response. This could alienate other members of the organisation and the public.

Sorting out your internal organisation is a vital first step in launching a publicity campaign. If you are more than a very small group, internal procedures for developing effective communication within the organisation will be necessary. If a number of different people are going to speak to the press, then they must all know what the others are saying. Also, what a press spokesman or woman says must be what the organisation's view is, not their own personal opinion. An organisation must develop policies agreed by the group as a whole, or by its committees, which can be quoted in statements to the press.

Most voluntary organisations of any size designate one person as press officer to get over this problem and do not allow all staff to speak to the press. This can work well, especially as an organisation gets larger and more structured; but everyone can speak to the press if there is proper, effective internal communication, including regular meetings and/or good management.

The press officer fulfils other functions too. He or she needs to keep their organisation informed and in touch with media coverage affecting issues close at hand. The press officer is also responsible for putting forward other people to speak to the press, be interviewed, or write an article; their job is to 'sell' that person. It is much easier to sell someone else as an expert on something or an excellent speaker/writer, etc. than it is to sell yourself. The press officer can also develop a closer relationship with individual journalists who are interested in that cause and this can be an important factor in getting good media coverage (see chapter 2).

It is a good idea to try to assess the response you get to each separate publicity exercise – the number of 'column inches' gained in the local or national press as the result of your initiative, and the amount of radio and TV coverage. This will enable you to judge whether the time and money that went into the exercise were justified. If, for example, you hold a press conference with the main aim to get publicity and you get very little, you should think about other ways to go about it. If you hold a conference for the benefit of staff, volunteers, etc. with publicity as a secondary aim, then obviously your priorities will be different.

## Your organisation's 'image'

The media deals in images, and before setting out to make your organisation better known you need to think about the image that you'd like to present to the world at large. Do you want to appear outspoken or dependable, old or young, aggressive or compassionate, political or apolitical? How will the way you present yourself affect your perceived image?

Everything about your dealings with the press will help to create your image. The kind of headed paper you send out, the style and presentation of your written material, the people who act as spokesmen and women and the organisation's attitudes over the telephone or face to face will all create an image in the mind of the press and public It is as well to be aware of this and make some conscious decisions, otherwise you might find yourself with an image that it may be very difficult to shake off later on.

## What is news?

If a voluntary organisation is to have successful dealings with the media, it will need to develop a sense of what is news and what is not. The media has its own news values, with which many people, and perhaps especially those working in voluntary organisations, do not agree. On the whole, journalists are looking for news where there is conflict or controversy, danger to the community, something unusual (i.e.. man bites dog), some scandal or some outstanding achievement or simply a piece of information which has never been published before.

Journalists are also interested in personalities as well as issues - the media frequently adopts a number of outspoken people who appear again and again despite the fact that there are many others with just as much to say. If you want to get media coverage, it is better on the whole to accept these news values and try to get your stories to fit in than to try to persuade the media to adopt your own values. However, because of this the *benefit* of successful media coverage may be at the *cost* of your organisations's other goals.

To avoid a lot of wasted time and effort, it is important to understand what is *not* news. Routine events - things that happen every day -are of little interest to journalists. So, although it may be terrible that thousands of handicapped babies are born every year, the media will not see this as news. However, news that a particular drug has caused handicap *will* be news, as it contains practically all the vital 'news ingredients' - conflict (between the drug company and the public and/or pressure groups), scandal (about the drug company), danger to the community, and something new which has been revealed.

But the fact that thousands of handicapped babies are born every year can be made news if some new campaign is launched to do something about it, if some well-known personality has a handicapped baby and publicises their plight, or if a particularly successful fund-raising event has taken place.

There is a considerable difference, of course, between national news and local news. Just as many voluntary organisations *over*-estimate their newsworthiness in the national context, so do many *under*-estimate their appeal to the local media. The head of one local independent radio station, addressing a seminar organised by a council for voluntary service to help its member organisations to learn to use the local media, said:

> Remember that we need you to provide us with news as much as you need us to reach your clients. We want local stories, and I would estimate that about 80-90 per cent of the local news that comes into us is used. What I want to ask you people here is: if we haven't heard of you before, why not? If you're starting a new organisation, launching a campaign, opening a new centre, holding a sponsored event, then that's news, and we want to hear from you.

To get news coverage, then, you need to fit your stories into the news values accepted by the media as a whole, and to clarify whether this will have more than local interest. If you find it isn't possible to write it up as 'news', then it's worth questioning whether it's worth sending out that particular press release or contacting that journalist.

# The published media

### NATIONAL PRESS
The national press falls into two main groups – the 'quality' press and the 'popular' press. The 'quality' press – the *Daily Telegraph, Financial Times, The Guardian, The Independent* and *The Times* – have a much smaller readership than the popular press – the *Daily Mirror, Sun, Today, Daily Star, Daily Express* and *Daily Mail*. But the people who read the quality press are the people who on the whole have greater power and influence – politicians, businessmen, public figures.

If you want to get your message across to the public at large, then a couple of column inches in the *Sun* are worth more than a long article in *The Times*. If, however, you are campaigning for changes in government policy, or asking businessmen to donate to your organisation, then the quality press is the better place. There is often more space for long or reflective in-depth pieces in the quality Sunday papers. Many papers also carry a health page, women's page, and education pages which are likely to carry articles on issues of concern to voluntary groups.

The table below shows circulation figures for the national press. Two other papers are also worth considering – the *Morning Star*, which – although it has a circulation of only 15,000 – does carry articles on voluntary organisations and pay attention to many of the issues that concern them, and London's *The Evening Standard*, which – although strictly a local paper – is read by many people with influence in the capital and Home Counties.

| Audit Bureau Circulation Figures | |
|---|---|
| Title | Average net sales June-November 1990 |
| *Popular dailies* | |
| Sun | 3,893,282 |
| Daily Mirror/Record | 3,903,252 |
| Daily Mail | 1,704,633 |
| Daily Express | 1,599,240 |
| Daily Star | 925,900 |
| Today | 552,931 |
| *Quality dailies* | |
| Daily Telegraph | 1,078,084 |
| The Times | 424,051 |
| The Guardian | 423,155 |
| The Independent | 411,626 |
| Financial Times | 290,032 |
| London Evening Standard | 505,579 |
| *Popular Sundays* | |
| News of the World | 5,073,946 |
| Sunday Mirror | 2,920,482 |

| Sunday People | 2,583,244 |
| Mail on Sunday | 1,910,633 |
| Sunday Express | 1,678,035 |
| | |
| *Quality Sundays* | |
| Sunday Times | 1,161,485 |
| Sunday Telegraph | 593,459 |
| The Observer | 548,359 |
| Independent on Sunday | 343,786 |

*Source:* ABC

## REGIONAL AND LOCAL PRESS

Most towns have local newspapers, usually published once a week, and there are a number of large local and regional daily papers too. You can find out the circulation of your local papers, whether they are for sale or free, what sort of people read them, and what their deadlines are either by approaching the papers direct or using one of the press guides such as *Willings, Benns* and *Brad* (see Useful Publications). All types of people read local papers because most people are interested in local affairs.

Many of these local papers are owned by large newspaper groups such as the Westminster Press, Thompsons and the Mirror Group. These groups provide a syndication service (news distribution service) to their newspapers, so it is sometimes worth sending a press release to the central office of the newspaper group (see *Brad, Benn* or *Willings*) and letting them do the work of sending it out to all their papers.

## COMMUNITY NEWSPAPERS

A relatively new development has been the increased interest in producing community newspapers. These are often produced by a team of enthusiastic volunteers, some of whom have journalistic experience and some not, and aim to cover the news and views of the local community in a new way, avoiding many of the clichés and news values of conventional journalism. Some local councils and churches also produce local newspapers with a community feel about them, and often these have free 'events' columns.

## TRADE AND SPECIALIST PRESS

Apart from newspapers, there is a vast range of magazines covering almost every subject and every interest group. Apart from well-known magazines such as the main women's magazines which retail in every newsagent, there are a large number of trade and specialist publications. Almost every profession has a magazine aimed at it: for example, social workers have *Community Care* (circulation 26,000 in 1990) published by IPC (International Publishing Corporation, one of the largest magazine publishers in the country), doctors have *Medical News, Pulse* and a wide range of specialist medical magazines, and so on. There are a number of 'political' magazines which may carry articles on subjects of interest to voluntary organisations. The *New Statesman & Society*, with a circulation of about 32,000 in 1990, carries some articles of the sort which appeared in the old *New Society*. *The Spectator* (circulation 40,000 in 1990), might be also worth considering, or *The Economist* might carry articles on social policy from time to time.

## THE 'RADICAL' PRESS

The last 20 years or so have seen the rise – and many cases fall – of a large number of 'radical' or 'alternative' publications, such as *The Leveller, Oz, Rolling Stone* and *Vole*.

Some, like *Gay News, Private Eye* and *Spare Rib*, have been very successful and have achieved high circulation figures. Others, like *Time Out* in London, have succeeded but become straight commercial operations. Some of these publications offer free listings to suitable organisations. Some may serve a specialised readership not easily reached through conventional publications.

## THE ETHNIC MINORITY PRESS

There are also a number of newspapers and magazines for Britain's ethnic minorities. Some of these, like the *Asian Times, Caribbean Times* and *The Voice*, all weeklies, have a high readership and voluntary organisations would do well to consider using them. The Commission for Racial Equality, Elliot House, 10-12 Allington Street, London SW1E 5EH, produces a list of the Ethnic Minority Press in Britain.

## NEWS AGENCIES

The Press Association is Britain's only national news agency, and is owned by the provisional newspaper groups. PA provides a constant stream of news via telex to every newspaper and broadcasting station in the country.

Other news agencies which you are likely to have heard of, such as Reuters and UPI (United Press International), provide international news.

# The broadcasting media

## NATIONAL RADIO

BBC national radio consists of five 'channels', Radios 1, 2, 3 and 4 and the newly created Radio 5, which is mainly children's and educational programmes and sport. There are also Radio Scotland, Wales and Northern Ireland. News bulletins on all of these are produced by BBC Radio News, although independent teams put together the news and current affairs for programmes such as 'Today'(Radio 4), 'You and Yours' (Radio 4), 'Newsbeat' (Radio 1) and 'Woman's Hour' (Radio 4). A unit within BBC Radio News provides a network news service for the BBC local radio stations. Each radio channel offers a wide range of programmes –current affairs, documentary, drama, discussion programmes –which may be of interest to voluntary organisations.

The BBC also broadcasts overseas in English and in about 40 foreign languages through its External Services at Bush House, Strand, London WC2 4PH. If your organisation has overseas programmes, External Services are likely to be interested in hearing about them.

At the moment there is no independent, commercial national radio station in Britain, but IRN -Independent Radio News - operates from the offices of the London Broadcasting Company (LBC) in London. IRN provide national news bulletins to almost all the independent local radio stations in Britain. The first national commercial radio station will start broadcasting by late autumn 1992.

## LOCAL RADIO

BBC local radio began in 1967 when eight pilot radio stations were set up as a two-year experiment. In 1969, the Government endorsed this as a success and the BBC decided that local radio would be financed out of an increased licence fee. The BBC was given the go-ahead to expand, and at present there are some 38 local BBC radio stations in England (at the end of 1990). There are also four 'opt-out' stations in Wales, eight in Scotland and two in Northern Ireland.

In 1967, pirate radio stations –launched with Radio Caroline in 1964 –were made illegal, and the BBC moved in to 'fill the gap' with Radio 1. However, the success of the pirate stations showed that commercial radio could work and a Government White Paper on commercial radio was published in 1971. This required independent local radio – ILR – to be truly a public service rather than simply a vehicle for advertising. It would be under the control of the Independent Broadcasting Authority (IBA) which also controlled independent television.

The first commercial radio station opened in London in 1973. By 1982 there were 34. By the end of the 1980s some 50 independent local radio stations could be heard by about 90 per cent of the country's population. By the end of 1990 there were another 23 'incremental' radio contracts which were granted by the Independent Broadcasting Authority before the Broadcasting Act became law in November 1990.

## OTHER RADIO

In addition to these broadcast services, there are other radio stations which transmit their material by cable. These include hospital radio services, of which there were around 300 serving about 80 per cent of hospitals in 1982, and student radio stations, which operate from university campuses. Some of these audiences may be target groups for voluntary organisations and should not be forgotten.

Community radio provides another alternative to the present 'duopoly' of BBC and independent stations. There are a few community radio stations which distribute their programmes via cable rather than over the air.

Community radio is radio that is owned, managed and made by its audience. In other countries it is already a reality; in Australia, for example, there are over 70 non-profit stations providing a range of services not provided by the national and commercial broadcasters. A typical Australian community radio's schedule might include several hours from an adult education college, a daily show made by school

11

children, a single parent's request show, coverage of district council debates, a half-hour of comedy from the town prison, and programmes made by local churches and political groups.

A two-year experiment in community radio was launched in 1985, with 266 applications being received for just 21 licences, but was abandoned in 1986 when the government planned wider changes to broadcasting. Radio TM, formerly Radio Thamesmead, had already started broadcasting and still operates as a genuine community radio station on an elderly cable network. In January 1988 it was announced that several hundred community radio stations are planned; these are becoming a reality in the 1990s.

Some 'pirate' community radio stations do operate. There are also a number of radio workshops scattered around the country - such as the London Radio Workshop, the Islington Radio Project or Sheffield's Commonsound - which help to train people to make radio programmes, and produce tapes and cassettes for a variety of purposes. For example, tapes can be made for broadcast on local radio. It is very unlikely that the BBC will ever use these tapes -they prefer to handle the production themselves.

## TELEVISION -NATIONAL AND REGIONAL

The BBC -BBC1 and BBC 2 -and ITV have national and regional programming. The major news and current affairs programmes will be 'networked' - that is, shown throughout the country. However, a certain amount of regional programming exists to provide local news and local current affairs programmes as well as films and drama. Some local and regional news will be broadcast every day, usually following a national news programme. Channel 4, SC4 (Wales) and TV-am do not have regional programming.

BBC Television News supplies the news for BBC1 and BBC2 nationally. Independent Television News - ITN - provides news nationally to the ITV regions. Channel 4 and TV-am have their own news-gathering services.

There are 11 BBC regional stations in England, four in Scotland, three in Wales and one in Northern Ireland. Each of these will produce their own regional news programmes and a number of special programmes.

ITV has 16 regional companies in the UK. These produce their own regional news and current affairs programmes, but also make a wider variety of special programmes, many of which will be on themes of interest to voluntary organisations and community groups.

Different departments exist within the BBC, ITV and Channel 4 to cover such areas as educational broadcasting, news and current affairs, and access programmes. If you want to do more than simply get 'news' across, you will need to look into these areas (see chapters 5, 6 and 7).

BBC World Service Television news was launched in March 1991, transmitting via Satellite or terrestrial links to the parts of Europe covered by the BBC Europe channel - Scandinavia, parts of France and Italy. It also goes to large parts of Eastern Europe. In October 1991 the Service went 24 hours to vast areas of South-east Asia by satellite, and also to the Gulf. It is based at the BBC Television Centre.

# 2
# Running A Press Office

Whether you are a small group of volunteers working from home, or have enough staff to set up a separate press office within your office accommodation, you will have to be well organised if you want to deal with the media successfully. Before you become involved in press work, you need to have some basic information and office equipment at your fingertips.

First of all, you need to draw up a list of the names, addresses and telephone numbers of relevant newspapers, magazines, radio and TV companies and programmes, both at local and national level. These should include the names of the individual journalists you need to contact. Find out who the relevant correspondent is - health, social services, home affairs, financial, consumer, education, women's issues, politics -and the news and features editors. You should also cover the specialist magazines likely to deal with your subject, and any local or community newspapers and newsletters. A list of freelance journalists interested in your subject -who might be able to persuade someone to publish an article on that theme - is also invaluable. The National Union of Journalists produces a freelance directory.

There are agencies who will do a lot of basic press work for you -supplying press lists, printing and mailing out press releases - but these are too expensive for all but the larger voluntary organisations to make use of (see Useful Addresses). There are also a number of press directories which are updated regularly – *Benns* and *Willings* come out once a year, and *Pims* and *PR Planner* are updated monthly. Details of these and their cost are given in the list of Useful Publications – but it makes sense for the small voluntary organisation to copy out relevant entries from the copy in their public library or from a friendly organisation which already has this information.

Try to have all the information you are likely to need at your fingertips. Nothing is worse for a journalist who is writing a story than to ring up and find you talking at length about 'need' and 'urgency' without having the facts and figures to back it up. Prepare a file of all the relevant information, such as what the issue is, who is affected by it, what the existing legislation is and what your organisation is doing. Keep a file of relevant press cuttings so that you know what has been written about your subject and from what angle. File these where you can find them quickly – a journalist may ring up saying 'There was a report in one of the papers about three weeks ago saying...' and you need to be able to lay your hands on it straight away.

Most large press offices receive the national papers, magazines and journals which are likely to carry the stories their organisations are interested in, as well as report on their own work. This can be expensive – a way round it is to ask all staff to buy and bring in a different daily newspaper, or to find a way of scanning papers and periodicals that you can't afford. There are specialist cuttings agencies (see Useful Addresses) which will scan all the local and regional press throughout the country, and also cover specialist magazines at your request, but again, these are expensive and often the cuttings are very repetitive as a story may be repeated in different papers which belong to the same chain.

It helps to keep a record of all press calls: who made them, which paper/radio/TV, what time, what it was about. This should be done automatically whenever anyone in the organisation talks to a journalist; that way important messages won't get lost and you will also have some record of what went on. Nothing is worse than a journalist talking to several different people in an organisation and getting several different responses. It may be worth printing special forms for this purpose.

If you keep a log of press calls, you will be able to look back over a campaign or over a year's work and see which media called you most often, which issues were the most interesting for the press, and so on. This may help you plan your publicity in the future.

It is a good thing to build up a reputation with the press for being experts on a particular issue. Then, every time a journalist is writing a piece about this issue – whether it's some aspect of housing, community care, poverty, discrimination – he or she will ring up to get facts, figures and a quote. If you are always available, have the facts to hand and are prompt and helpful, then the media will come to you.

You could also keep a list of friendly 'experts', people who are well known and who are prepared to speak on your behalf – doctors, legal experts, local councillors, for example – or of people who are suffering from whatever problem it is that you are trying to alleviate. If you can put journalists in touch with these people, it will help them to build up their 'story'.

Caroline Oliver, Divisional Director of Communications at Age Concern England, points out the responsibilities of an organisation towards its clients when journalists want to interview them.

> Elderly people are often very reluctant to speak to the press – if they say they will, they must be happy about it and know what they're letting themselves in for. You must find out whether they really want to do it or whether they are doing it because they feel obliged to an organisation which has helped them.

The following is an example of how this can go wrong. An elderly woman in south London on a state pension, plus a small private pension which had been eroded by inflation, agreed to appear on radio to say how hard she found it to make ends meet. She appeared under her own name but with no details of where she lived. The local paper, however, heard the interview and reproduced some of it, looked up her name in the telephone book and published her full name and address without contacting her. She then received an astonishing number of abusive letters and telephone calls. Caroline Oliver concludes:

> You must make sure what journalists want and check how closely people are to be identified. This is especially important with vulnerable groups such as old people. If you explain why, journalists will usually understand why remaining unidentified might be important.

# Dealing with journalists

Many people starting out with a small voluntary organisation who have had no experience of press work feel inhibited about speaking to journalists. The press, radio and television appear a glamorous world and journalists are always busy and often appear offhand. If you ring them up and they are in the middle of writing an article for a deadline in half an hour, it is not surprising that their attitude is 'Yes, what are you ringing me about? Get to the point.'

Normally you shouldn't contact a journalist unless you have something specific to say. If you are launching a new organisation or campaign, then that's fine – you have something to say. But what if your organisation is doing useful work and you are not getting the kind of publicity you need to further your aims and expand your range of clients, volunteers or supporters. How do you improve your relationship with the media?

To begin with, you can get to know your local journalists, or, if your organisation or campaign has national coverage, the relevant correspondents on the national press. It is normal for a new press officer taking over a large and well-established voluntary organisation which gets a fair amount of media coverage to ring up and announce themselves just to establish their presence, often after sending out a press release. This obviously won't work if you are a small and unknown group, but you can find other ways to get in touch.

One way is to ask if speakers from the local press, radio or TV stations can come along and address a meeting of your organisation or of your clients and talk about their work. Even better, a number of voluntary organisations could get together and invite speakers to a 'media workshop' where they can find out more about their local media and how to use it. Most local papers, radio and TV are well aware that the voluntary sector can provide them with good stories and many local radio and TV stations have 'community projects' staff who are interested in building links with local groups. Such initiatives involve a lot of organisation but can be worth it all in terms of their results – face-to-face contact with local journalists in a more relaxed setting, and a greater knowledge of how the media work.

Whatever your cause, you have a lot to gain by interesting a particular journalist in the issue so that he or she can fight the battle to get an article or news report into a paper on your behalf. However, journalists do tend to change jobs fairly frequently so keeping in touch with them is a never-ending task. You may find you have just got somebody sympathetic to your cause when they leave the paper and you have to start all over again.

Getting in touch with the media over a specific issue is usually done by sending out a press release – though getting in touch with local radio is often done less formally (see chapter 3). However, you are not always the ones to initiate contact – sometimes the journalist will approach you in connection with a piece he or she is researching. Talking to the press can make people very nervous – most people are afraid that they will be misquoted.

Many of the fears voluntary organisations have in this respect are well founded. A journalist is likely to paraphrase what you say in a more concise form which may not reflect the subtleties of your speech. When speaking to the press, it is worth expressing yourself as simply and bluntly as possible to avoid this danger. However, most people's image of the media is coloured by the high-powered interviews seen on radio and TV where the journalists are trying to catch their interviewee out. Politicians, union representatives and other public figures are seasoned performers and fair game for this kind of thing, but the average voluntary organisation isn't. At a local level, the press are likely to be friendly and willing to help you to get your message across. Only if you are involved in some controversial or overtly political activity are you likely to be given a difficult time.

If you are courteous and helpful to the press they are likely to be the same towards you – but hostility breeds hostility. However, there is a big difference between journalists on the so-called 'quality' papers, and those on the popular tabloids. The first category is more likely to want the 'truth', the second is more interested in sensation. The popular papers can reach millions of people, and are worth cultivating – but there are times when it is better to avoid making approaches to them.

When talking to a journalist, it is sometimes a useful device to speak 'off the record'. This involves taking the journalist into your confidence. You may wish to give information which cannot be reported for one reason or another (if only because it would embarrass you!) but which would give the journalist a clearer understanding of the subject. Or you may wish something to be said, but not attributed to you. In this case you could give the journalist clues to ask someone else the right questions. It is absolutely essential that you and the journalist agree beforehand when comments are to be treated as 'off the record'. If this is not made explicit, then the journalist has every right to use and attribute everything you say.

When you are talking over the telephone you may get carried away and say more than you mean. Journalists know that this is less likely to happen in a face-to-face encounter and will often encourage you to go on at great length over the telephone if they're looking for sensitive information. In these circumstances you must use your discretion; try to visualise the story in print. Another ploy is to talk 'off the record' and explain the issue in question as honestly and realistically as possible.

Many people are so eager to talk to the press that they don't give themselves time to think about what they want to say. If a journalist rings up and you want to give some thought to your reply, then ask if you can call back in five or ten minutes, but do prepare your answer and get together any facts you need to back it up. If you are asked something you don't know, never waffle or give unfounded opinions or speculations; say you'll check and ring back quickly. And if you remember something you ought to have said after you've put the phone down, don't be afraid to ring back.

If you have been involved in work with radio, it is worth having a portable radio available in the office, or even better, a portable radio/cassette recorder so that you can record your organisation's representative while on the air. This is invaluable for learning how to interview well, and also gives you some permanent record of what was said. Better-off organisations who have access to video can also make videotapes of TV interviews.

If you are likely to do a lot of work with the media and have no previous experience, then it is worth considering some kind of training. There are a number of organisations which offer training courses in various aspects of using the media; these are listed in Useful Addresses.

# 3
# Putting Out a Press Release

Press releases are the bread and butter of the press officer's work. A press release – or news release – is simply a statement put out to the press summarising a story and telling the journalist where to go for further information. A good press release should save the journalist some work and put him or her onto a story. Sometimes press releases will simply be used verbatim, especially if they have summarised the news succinctly and given all the relevant facts.

To put out a press release you need a typewriter and some form of duplicator or photocopier. You can also have it printed – but, especially when you are dealing with local media, what you are saying is more important than the format you use. Some local – and even some national –media may be suspicious of a press release that appears too slick and too well packaged. They already get too many releases like this from commercial companies trying to 'invent' news for marketing purposes.

It will help to have an eye-catching headed paper with the name and symbol of your organisation to identify it among the dozens of other releases on a journalist's overcrowded desk. This effect can be double-edged. If you regularly send out good quality information, then being easily recognisable will be an advantage. Equally, however, if you regularly put out press releases which are not really news, your headed paper will help put the journalist off.

Only ever type on one side of the paper –standard A4 size is best. Staple any additional sheets together. This is because journalists will find it easier to cut and paste the press release into the story they are writing, and also because 'copy' sent to be typeset is always on one side only. Your press release should also be typed double-spaced with wide margins down each side to allow room for the journalist to make alterations and give instructions to the typist or printer. Examples 1 and 2 show how to write and present, and how *not* to write and present, a press release. At the top or the bottom of the press release you should give the date; at the top, a simple headline which should tell the reader immediately what the press release is about. Don't try to be too clever – leave this to the journalist.

Because newspapers and broadcasting stations are usually inundated with press releases, your first paragraph should grab the journalist's attention and summarise the whole story –otherwise he or she may look no further. The rule is that the first paragraph should always say the five 'Ws' – what, who, when, where, and why – though not necessarily in that order. It also helps to limit this first paragraph to a maximum of 40 words. You can then go on and say 'how' and give some of the background.

For example:

A sponsored fast [what] is to be held by 500 schoolchildren [who] at the offices of the Starving Children's Fund [where] on Saturday 14 June [when]. The fast is in aid of children suffering because of the recent drought in Pakistan [why].

The fast has been organised as one of a series being held up and down the country. Proceeds will go to the special International Drought in Pakistan Fund which is working on the spot to alleviate the crisis [how].

Far too often many organisations send out press releases whether or not they have any news. This often applies to larger organisations which feel they must mention every change of chairman, every AGM and every new policy which is passed, even if these have no obvious importance to other people. The attitude often seems to be: 'If we send out enough stuff, something might get used.' In fact, this approach is often counter-productive. Journalists will get used to seeing your headed paper, groan 'Oh no, not another from them', and put it straight into the bin, where about 70 per cent of press releases end up anyway.

This should not be the case with most voluntary organisations, however. The work of most voluntary bodies can be of interest either to the local community or the public at large. Often there is some controversy behind the work. Never be afraid to stress controversial aspects of a campaign; these will help you get good coverage and put your case across. If you put out press releases judiciously, when you know there really *is* news, then they should be used almost very time.

It is a good policy – and in any case will be necessary for a voluntary organisation with a small budget – not to send out a press release to too many newspapers, magazines, etc. Select the key local press and radio, try the nationals if the story is newsworthy from a national angle, and don't forget specialist magazines in your field.

A press release should never be very long – if you can fit it on to one side of A4 paper, typed double spaced, perfect. Otherwise, two pages are normally enough. If it is two pages, don't end the first page in mid-sentence. You should also say 'continued' or 'more' if it goes on to a second page. Telephone numbers where the journalists can get further information should always be given at the bottom – day-time numbers and night-time numbers should both be given if possible, as many journalists work late. If someone is only available at certain times, then put this at the bottom; if the journalist spends half the morning ringing a number because you haven't said the office will only be manned in the afternoon, then by the time you're there they may well have given up and be following up another story.

You should use very simple and straightforward language in writing a press release. Don't use jargon which presumes some knowledge of your specialist field; never use acronyms (strings of initials) without spelling out what they mean first time round; avoid long sentences; avoid clichés; don't use long-winded phrases like 'in spite of the fact that' (say 'although'), or 'on account of the fact that' (say 'because').

Use the active rather than the passive voice: 'Families in Crisis is launching a new campaign' is more effective than 'A new campaign is to be launched by Families in Crisis', and 'The group's chairman

# LANCASTER CHILDREN'S CARE ASSOCIATION

2 Market Square, Lancaster

## P R E S S    R E L E A S E

### FREE HOLIDAYS FOR CHILDREN IN CARE

Lancashire's thousand children in care are to be offered the holiday of a life-time as part of a new £15,000 project run by the Lancaster Children's Care Association.

The project, announced today (Monday 14 June), will rely on help provided by more than a thousand local adults who will act as special foster families for the children on holiday.

The two-week holidays, booked and paid for by LCCA, can be taken in any location in the British Isles.

LCCA Chairman Mr David Right said that the holiday project was an exciting step forward in introducing short-term fostering for all children in care in the county. 'We have campaigned long and hard for alternatives to residential care for children. Many of these children rarely get an opportunity to travel or even enjoy the briefest of holidays,' he said today.

Mr Right added: 'I am amazed at the public's response to our invitation last month for potential foster parents. The number volunteering help has not only made the project possible but also highlighted the general concern about children in care felt by ordinary families throughout Lancashire.'

### ENDS

EDITORS PLEASE NOTE:

The Lancaster Children's Care Association is a voluntary organisation set up 52 years ago to provide foster care for unwanted children in the area.

FOR FURTHER INFORMATION:

| Mr David Right | (Office) | (Home) |
|---|---|---|
| Chairman | (444) 666 999 | (444) 555 333 |
| Lancaster Children's Care Association | | |

Date release mailed: Monday 14 June 1991

Example 1

Lancaster Children 's
Care Association 2
Market Square Lancaster

Press Release

LCCA is a voluntary body with links to all child care agencies in the county. It is always looking for increased donations in the hope of expanding its work in the future into new and more challenging areas having been set up 52 years ago to provide care for unwanted children in the area. It is looking at new ways of approaching the issues of adoption, fostering and residential care for all children who need this at a local level. LCCA sees its role as being critical of local services where these fall short as well as providing alternative forms of care where necessary.

On Monday 21 May the Management Group of LCCA which is chaired by Mr D Right and which also includes Miss Elizabeth Batch and Johnny Bickerstaff decided to use LCCA funds to set up a project whereby all children in the region will be offered holidays with foster families for 2 weeks during the year ahead. Because of the recent response to a campaign asking for volunteer foster parents to look after children on holiday, all of the 1,000 children in care locally will be able to have a holiday, which is wonderful news for all these children many of whom seldom have the opportunity of even a short holiday and is a new departure for the LCCA.

Example 2

condemned the new policy' is better than 'This new policy was condemned by the group's chairman.'

Press releases often include a direct quote from the director or chairman of the organisation which will make it sound more lively. Quotes allow forceful opinions to be put across which would look odd in straight prose. For instance:

UVAC believes that the local government's failure to take action is a shocking example of...

is less effective than writing:

UVAC's chairman, Michael Gray, said today 'The local government's failure to act is a shocking example of...

Journalists often like quotes because it looks as though they have been talking to someone direct even if they don't have the time to do this, and helps to flesh out their article. Facts and figures also go down well in a press release; they can make the news sound more solid and again, make the journalists look as if they've done their work thoroughly.

## Embargoing a press release

An embargo is laid down when the press release clearly states at the top: NOT TO BE USED BEFORE (TIME) ON (DAY & DATE IN FULL). Its purpose is to enable you to send out news some time in advance of when you want the media to use it, e.g. for the publication of a report. This gives journalists a chance to prepare the story in advance if they want to, and to produce a more thoughtful, in-depth result.

The use of embargoes on press releases is a much misunderstood subject. People often seem to believe that they will make a press release somehow intrinsically more exciting if they issue it with an embargo. In reality, the opposite is usually true. Nothing causes more frustration to a journalist than an unnecessary embargo. The rule should be: use embargoes as sparingly as possible.

An obvious example of where an embargo is necessary is sending out the text of a speech which is to be made the following day –by sending it out in advance you will get better coverage. You cannot embargo something that has actually happened, like a meeting, a conference or a demonstration.

Embargoes are almost always respected, unless they are used cynically to prevent the news from being covered effectively (e.g. if an unpopular report is to be released, embargoing it till Budget Day, when there will be less space in the papers to cover it).

Embargoes can go wrong. If you send out the text of a speech in advance and the speaker is taken ill, or if you give details of an event that for some reason had to be postponed or never took place, you could look very silly. For example, one local MIND group sent out an embargoed release on a court case relevant to their work which was coming up the following morning. But the case was rescheduled at the last minute and they had to ring round all the local media telling them not to use the press release.

If there is no good reason to embargo, then it's much safer not to – just put out the press release marked 'for immediate use'. Always date it.

# Deadlines

To use an embargo effectively you need to know something about the 'deadlines' which journalists work to. To get a news story into a morning daily paper you would have to have a very important item to get coverage of anything submitted after five o'clock the previous evening. For an evening paper, it should be not later than twelve noon or one o'clock. Weekly newspapers publish on different days, and you should find out the publication days of your local weeklies and then work back one day, i.e. you should submit a new item first thing on Thursday for a paper which comes out on Friday. For weeklies, the earlier in the production week you get your press release in, the more chance that they'll use it – but on the less important inside pages.

Deadlines are not so important for broadcasting stations, as they produce several news bulletins and magazine programmes daily. However, if you are aiming for a particular slot or news programme, you should again get your news in well in advance. For the BBC, either radio or TV, it is very important for press releases to arrive on the Wednesday for use in the following week's programme. In other words, a release embargoed for a Thursday should already be circulating with the BBC on the previous Wednesday, eight days earlier.

You can use an embargo, therefore, to pick the media coverage you want for a particular piece of news or event. If you embargo a story for 00.30 hours you will get coverage in the morning media rather than the evening. If you embargo it for 12.00 noon, you are more likely to get coverage in the local evening paper and regional news-rooms, but will miss the local morning paper and breakfast-time radio, which is when radio has its biggest audience. If you are aiming for a particular programme, find out when you need to contact them: for example for the 'Today' programme on BBC Radio 4, the best time to ring through possible news ideas is between 11.30 a.m. and 12.00 noon, Monday to Friday.

Sunday is usually a day of few news events, so many voluntary - and other - organisations embargo a story for late on Sunday so that it can appear on Monday. However, Monday's paper is usually thinner than the other days precisely because news is short, and many voluntary organisations have the same idea!

## Whom to send it to

Many voluntary organisations make mistakes about whom to address a press release to, sending it, for example, to the managerial rather than editorial head of a paper or radio station or to the wrong journalist. You should send a press release to the special correspondent on the subject covered *and* to the news editor, or to the programme organiser where relevant.

The correspondent may be away covering another story, or on holiday, in which case the news editor will be the best person to deal with it. One local voluntary organisation sent a press release for a story, which would definitely have been used, to the Managing Director of Radio Hallam marked 'private and confidential'. He was on holiday and as a result, the sealed envelope waited on his desk till his return two weeks later, by which time the story was well and truly dead.

When you send the same press release to more than one person on the same paper, always make this known, if possible: write at the top of the news editor's copy 'separate copy sent to social services correspondent' and vice versa. This will alert them to the possibility of duplication of work - which, were it to happen, would create understandable feelings of irritation.

Sometimes it is worth following up a press release to ask if a journalist is going to cover the story or if they have received the release, but not as a matter of course. If it is newsworthy enough, it will get used whether you ring up or not. It may be best to follow up a press release only with those journalists you have already had contact with; you don't want to give unknown journalists the impression that you are hassling them.

# Giving an exclusive

If you have news which is best dealt with in some depth rather than in a couple of paragraphs, or information which would make the basis of a good feature article, you can give the story to a single newspaper or magazine as an exclusive. This will obviously make it a more attractive proposition to the publication concerned. With news, this may not in fact prevent other media picking up the story afterwards and dealing with it in brief; but it means you will have the chance of better coverage in one paper. This should be done with discretion, as overdoing it can alienate other papers.

Getting a feature written or placed is rather different from a news item, as usually there is no clear deadline. However, you may want the feature to come out on a particular day, for example to celebrate an anniversary or to coincide with the launching of a campaign. If you think you have information which would make a good feature, then ring up a journalist you know and discuss it with them.

There is nothing to stop someone within an organisation writing a feature and sending it in to the paper themselves, if they feel they can do justice to the issue better that way than by briefing a journalist. However, writing a journalistic article is a skill that many people do not have, and you should be aware of this. Nor should you be surprised if editors cut and rewrite parts of your article. This is normal even when an article is written by a professional journalist. However, it is quite legitimate – and a good precaution – to ask to be consulted about cuts or changes. You should always try to write more or less in the style of the paper concerned and keep to the same length as other features in the paper.

If you want to try writing yourself, it's worth ringing the features editor to see whether he or she would be interested in principle. They may well ask to see the article 'on spec', which means they have no obligation to publish it or pay you for it if they don't use it. If you are known to them and they have published something of yours before, they may commission you, which means they will pay a fee whether they use it or not.

## Using the Press Association

The Press Association - PA - is the only national news agency in Britain. It is owned by the Newspaper Society and provides a continuous stream of news material to all the provincial papers in Britain as well as to national papers, TV and radio.

Voluntary organisations can make use of PA by putting statements out through the agency, rather than by putting out a press release, or to complement a release sent out to major national and regional media. You can also make use of PA to release a statement that you may want to make in commenting on some wider issue which will be receiving media coverage.

What you do is to ring the newsdesk and talk to the news editor or to a specialist journalist who is likely to deal with your subject, and tell them what the story is. They may take details and write it up, or they may just suggest you transfer straight to 'copy' where a copytaker will take down the story or statement. It will then be edited and put out. This is unlikely to happen unless you have something which is genuinely of national importance, and if you are already known to PA.

## Getting publications reviewed

Many voluntary organisations issue publications and reports and want these to be reviewed or written up. As with all news releases, you have to have a realistic view of what is likely to receive news coverage and what is not. Sending out a press release or a report on a local project to national papers is silly; it would be far better to concentrate on the local angle, and perhaps call in a photographer to take a photograph of the project in action and have a brief caption story, rather than trying to get a report on the more academic issues which the project illustrates.

With more substantial publications, the specialist press are probably the best to seek reviews in. If a book is well reviewed in one of these, others may latch on. Do not be too ambitious: review space is strictly limited in most publications, and, in any case, a small voluntary organisation is not likely to be able to afford to send out a lot of free review copies, especially as it is often wise to send one paper or broadcasting station more than one copy.

# 4
# Holding a Press Conference

Holding a press conference, or a news conference as it might be more aptly named, is a way of encouraging journalists to cover a story in greater depth than might otherwise be the case. It is also a way of ensuring journalists get more of a 'feel' for your organisation, and meet representatives first hand. It also allows a convenient opportunity for photographers and broadcasters to get hold of the people they want to photograph or interview. However, journalists are very busy and are unlikely to come to a conference unless the story is important.

A press conference is often an 'event' in itself. It may get more coverage than a press release alone. On the other hand, the journalists may not come at all as it takes some time out of their day to get there and back. They may prefer simply to rely on a press release. When holding a press conference, therefore, you should always send out a release as well. It is also important that the speakers and members of your organisation be available for comment in the day or two before the conference to talk to those journalists not attending but still wanting to 'cover' the story.

Give at least 48 hours' notice of your press conference. If it is for a planned event, you can give as much as three or four weeks' notice. You will then need to send round some other notice - perhaps an embargoed press release - a day or two beforehand to remind journalists.

Planning the press conference need not take much time if you have some basic rules sorted out. First of all, you should check it is not going to clash with another conflicting event.

It is also important to have a realistic idea of the turnout and plan your conference accordingly: nothing is worse than a podium and speakers with microphones in a large hall if only two or three journalists turn up. It may be better just to sit around a large table or have a small meeting in someone's office: it will look better to have people crowded into a small space than looking lost in a large one.

However, you will need to have quiet offices or space nearby to give journalists and broadcasters a chance to carry out interviews; space for people to move around and talk to one another after the conference itself is over; and telephones for journalists to use.

The best time of day to hold a press conference for national media is in the morning, probably at around 11.00 or 11.30 a.m. This is the time when journalists are freest to leave their desks and least under pressure with deadlines. If you choose a Monday, the Sunday paper correspondents are unlikely to attend as it is their day off, but this will not matter if what you are saying is hot news. If you want the Sundays to come, though, another day is best. Fridays are a bad day, since Saturday papers tend to be read by fewer people.

As with an ordinary press release, when you send out the advance notice you need to say where, when, what it's about, who is speaking and why it's being held. These simple facts should be enough as the journalists are coming along to be filled in. It will obviously help if you can get a 'name' to speak at the press conference: you can invite a relevant MP or councillor to say something to give the news more weight.

Have a programme with fixed times and then stick to them.

## SAMPLE PROGRAMME

| | |
|---|---|
| 11.00 a.m. | start: introduction of speakers by chairman |
| 11.05 | first speaker |
| 11.15 | second speaker |
| 11.25 | questions |
| 11.35 | coffee |

It is a good idea to have the programme printed and handed out to the journalists when they arrive, but it is also important to make sure that the speakers stay within the time given. They should keep their speeches short –no more than about ten minutes each. The whole press conference should not normally take more than half an hour. Journalists are notorious for arriving late, but don't keep the ones who have already arrived waiting more than five minutes before you get started. The latecomers will soon pick up the thread. Allow plenty of time for journalists to ask questions at the end.

It is also a good idea to provide the journalists with a 'press kit' when they arrive. This will contain background information on your organisation, a copy of the press release you are putting out, copies of speeches and any other relevant information. But don't swamp them with a lot of irrelevant information.

When the journalists arrive, get them to write their names and who they represent on a piece of paper or in a press book; this will help you identify them and also give you a record of who come. If it is to be a large affair, you can also provide badges, both for yourselves and for the speakers and press, to help you identify one another. In a small informal conference this is not necessary.

Make sure that a press conference really is for the press; don't invite half your organisation and various worthies to come along and outnumber them, as happens at many voluntary organisation press conferences. The journalists will want to hear the facts, ask their questions, perhaps do an interview or two, and go away; they won't want to be cornered by a stray committee member and lectured about the work or your organisation as a whole. If there are other members of staff or volunteers there, then make sure they allow the journalists to ask their questions first and don't take over the proceedings.

However, in case no journalist asks a question, it can be worth asking a member of staff to ask one to get the ball rolling or the chairman can ask a speaker to elaborate on one point.

You would normally offer refreshment, but coffee and biscuits are sufficient for a voluntary organisation – the press *don't* always require alcoholic drinks, especially in the morning. If you serve coffee after the formal proceedings it may provide the opportunity for journalists and speakers to talk more informally afterwards. This is also the best time for radio journalists to record any interviews.

With the best planning in the world, a press conference is always something of an unpredictable affair. Sometimes there will be a good turnout for something which seems far less newsworthy than another conference which has a poor turnout. Sometimes you can isolate the reason why –the offices were too difficult to reach, the time of day was wrong, the issue was simply not presented interestingly enough. Sometimes, however, there may simply be too much other news happening on that day –and it will not be your fault if a major political leader dies or if the local town hall is burned down.

Finally, don't be tempted to overdo press conferences. The work of very few voluntary organisations will be sufficiently newsworthy to justify more than one or two a year.

# Planning a publicity event

Press conferences are not the only way of getting a message across to the press. Increasingly voluntary organisations have staged events which are intended to achieve the same thing, but also provide material suitable for visual coverage on television.

Demonstrations or rallies; the handing over of petitions or reports to the relevant government department, health authority or other body; all-night vigils – all can capture the press's, and the public's, imagination. Ordinary demonstrations, however, have become so common as to have lost much of their impact, and voluntary groups need to think carefully of ways of making them relevant and interesting. Demonstrations should of course always be non-violent, and if possible good-humoured. Banners or placards should convey well-thought-out slogans and the names of the organisations that are involved; photographs can be a great help.

A great deal of care needs to go into planning such events. You want to make sure that enough people will turn up, that the demonstration will be orderly, and that it will give a good impression of your organisation and the people who support it. Getting a local MP or other well-known figure to attend can help greatly in getting publicity, as well as making it more difficult for opponents to argue that you are 'just a group of hooligans'.

You also need to check that the timing of your event does not coincide with another, bigger event which could steal your fire. An example was in 1990 when the Disability Consortium planned a demonstration to campaign for improved rights and benefits for disabled people. They chose the same Saturday as the second major anti-Poll Tax demonstration. Although it was in the end featured briefly on the national TV news, it was inevitably covered in less detail than might otherwise have been expected.

Finally, you can use a rally or demonstration to get your message across to ordinary passers-by. Don't forget to take leaflets explaining the work of your organisation and the issue of the day, get people to sign petitions if relevant, or invite them to join your group.

# 5
# Interviews on Radio and Television

Radio and television are often thought to be the 'glamorous' side of the media. Voluntary organisations and the people who work for them feel that they have 'made it' when they appear on radio or television. It is certainly true that broadcasting has an immediacy and familiarity about it which is not usually the case with the written word, and there are opportunities for getting your message across in a friendly and approachable way.

It is also true that its coverage is often more superficial, and that news stories on radio and TV are necessarily shorter than in newspapers. Television, in particular, looks for black and white, easily dramatised issues, and tends either to disregard stories with nuances or get them wrong. Voluntary organisations often do better in a 'softer' slot such as BBC's 'Pebble Mill at One', or where a longer feature will enable the subtleties to be put across. In general, beware of television. It is above all a 'show-biz' medium and for this reason it is difficult for people who are used to dealing with matter-of-fact, practical affairs, to make best use of. On the other hand, of course, is the degree of exposure you will get, and the opportunity go get your organisation's name –even if nothing more –into almost every living-room in the land.

You will only be successful in developing this side of your work if you do the basic preparation and are aware of the pitfalls.

There are three main aspects of work with radio and television: the first is news coverage and interviews, through news and current affairs programmes. This is the main focus of this chapter. The second is inserts into magazine programmes, features, interviews, advice programmes, guests on opinion programmes, and broadcasting regular information in, for example, a local radio 'job slot' or diary. The third is putting across information in the wider variety of radio and television programmes - documentary, drama and drama-documentary, 'access' slots, educational programmes and appeals - as well as new options such as community service announcements. Special programmes - for example for the blind, elderly, ethnic minorities - may be particularly useful. All these areas will be dealt with in the following two chapters.

From time to time a voluntary organisation may be approached by the local radio or regional television and asked to appear on a certain programme, but mostly you will have to take the initiative yourself. This means sending out press releases when you have some news, getting in touch with journalists who work on programmes which you know will be interested in the kind of work you are doing, and listening to and watching what goes on so that you can take advantage of the opportunities that exist.

## Using local radio

Local radio stations are usually very approachable. Apart from the people on the news side - the news editor and reporters - local radio stations have someone called a programme organiser on a BBC station and a programme controller on an independent local radio (ILR) station, who make planning decisions. On a small station, very often it is the presenter of a particular programme who decides everything about what goes into their programme. All these people should be borne in mind when you want to get something about your organisation on the radio.

On the news side, local radio stations are often short of local news stories, and are also often short of staff -especially at weekends - which means that they are not always able to go out looking for good local material. This means that they are very likely to look at any local news which you send in, or listen if you telephone. One news editor of a local radio station in the North of England estimates that 80-90 per cent of local press releases sent in to his radio station are used. If you ring up or send in a press release for Saturday use you are quite likely to have someone call over the weekend to do an interview.

When using local radio, you must find out what programmes are produced, when they're broadcast, which are likely to be interested in the kind of stories you have, and which are the most popular with certain audiences. You can find out what times of day have the peak number of listeners in commercial radio stations simply by ringing up and asking them to send you their advertising rate card. From 8 a.m. to 9 a.m., a 30 second slot may cost £200, while at 3 a.m. the same 30 seconds might cost only £1.50. If you are appealing to insomniacs, the depressed and lonely, shiftworkers or the suicidal, that is worth bearing in mind.

The BBC will also have listenership figures for their stations, which you can also ask for. Most radio stations know what age-group listens in at what time, so if you're appealing to young people or elderly people, you can pick your slot accordingly.

Listen to local radio, be aware of that they offer. Try to think of alternative approaches. For example, you may want to get the problems of mentally handicapped people discussed, but there's no 'news' angle, and no one seems interested in slotting an interview into a magazine programme. However, there is a regular Church programme which is looking for good material. Why not use that, with an appropriate angle: 'The mentally handicapped - does the Church care?'

If you hear an interview on local radio which you disagree with and want to reply to, then ring in at once and say who you are and what you want to say. Radio stations are always looking for controversy and for alternative views. They also have a duty imposed on them by the BBC or the Independent Television Commission to be 'balanced', so you may be asked in to do a follow up.

## National radio

Using national radio is obviously rather different. They will be interested mainly in news which is of national significance. You are unlikely to get the same kind of interest in 'community' type issues as you are through local radio stations, many of which will have a specific policy of encouraging links with the community. However, many voluntary organisations and their causes do make news and features and if it comes to being interviewed, many of the same points will apply whether you are being interviewed for a local or national audience.

# Before the interview

If you are asked to do a radio or TV interview there are several things you should be clear about in advance:

1   What is the programme?
2   What information do they have, *why* the interview, do they have your press release?
3   What are you likely to be asked about and how long will you be given to talk?
4   Will it go out live or be pre-recorded? If pre-recorded, is it possible for them to come and record or film in your own office?
5   Who is the best person in your organisation to do the interview?

These five points may seem obvious, but it is surprising how many people will jump at the opportunity of doing an interview before thinking through the essential questions.

Dealing with these five points in order:

1   Listen to or watch the programme you are going to appear on so that you are aware of the presenter's style, roughly how long you will be given to speak, and the kinds of questions that are asked. It is also worth finding out who the programme's normal audience is.
2   It is important to check with the programme editor what information they have already received. You could suggest they see a recent report, for example, which may assist them to plan the interview and questions. It is also necessary to find out *why* the interview is taking place at all. Does it stem from your organisation's initiative, or is it to coincide with another event or statement on which you are being asked to comment?
3   Before the interview, you will often be given a chance to talk to the presenter or an assistant. This will enable you to find out what you will be asked and run through the replies. Interviewers will seldom give all the exact questions as this can remove

spontaneity from the interview and make the replies seem flat and dull. If you are new to radio or TV, it is most unlikely that anyone will try and 'catch you out' as they would an experienced politician. On the contrary, they will want to give you every help in order that it will be a good interview.

A news editor for a local BBC radio station, giving a talk to a group of representatives of voluntary organisations, said that the interviewer always wanted to stay on the side of the listener. So, if the person interviewed is evasive, negative, bigoted, or doesn't seem to know what they're talking about, the interviewer becomes hostile. If, on the other hand, the person interviewed is honest, straightforward, and has some warmth and concern, then the interviewer becomes sympathetic. This will tend to happen irrespective of whether the interviewer actually agrees with his or her point of view.

On radio, you can have in front of you a list of vital points you want to get across, perhaps also some facts and figures to back you up. Take care that you don't rustle the paper too near the microphone – you can write notes on stiff card to avoid this problem, and never read from a text –this will make your voice sound flat and boring, and you will also lose contact with the interviewer. If you actually talk to the interviewer, this will make the best impact with the listener too.

4    If the interview is to be pre-recorded, try to get them to come to you, if possible. You will be more relaxed in your own surroundings than in a studio and may well have more chance to talk over the interview beforehand. If it's pre-recorded, then whether you're in the office or the studio, you have an opportunity to get things exactly right. If you've made an error or feel you've expressed something badly, just say, 'I'm sorry, I got that wrong,' and do it again.

The disadvantage of pre-recording is that the tape can be edited in the studio before going out. This means that what you say can be altered –for instance, long-winded qualifying phrases can be cut so that your replies may seem stronger than you would prefer, or parts of the interview that you would prefer to have been broadcast can be cut and less important parts retained. However, the purpose of editing is not to make someone appear to say the opposite of what was intended. Skilful editing can sharpen up a somewhat woolly interview, cut out long pauses and unwanted 'ums' and 'ers', and make it sound as if both interviewer and interviewee were quick and on their toes.

If you are appearing on television, being filmed in hour office gives you an opportunity to present the image of your organisation to the public. It is important to pay attention to the background: books or effective posters can look good, while bare walls or faded postcards will look awful. If you are filmed at a desk, a clean one may make it look as if you've got no work to do, but one piled high with papers and files may make the office look inefficient! For television be aware of annoying mannerisms: don't hide your face, or pat your hair.

If the interview is live –whether in the radio or TV studio –it is even more important to be properly briefed. However, if you haven't done an interview before, try not to get too nervous, as it's very rare for anyone to completely 'fluff' an interview. People going to do live interviews for the first time are always afraid that they will dry up completely or forget what they meant to say, but they underestimate the professionalism of the interviewer who, if he or she sees that you are losing your way, will chip in with a quick question that will immediately put you back on course. To prove how effective this technique is, have you actually ever heard someone suddenly dry up on the radio or suddenly announce 'I've forgotten what I was saying?' except perhaps on a phone-in programme?

5 Be realistic about who will come over well on radio or TV. Some people, no matter how knowledgeable, will always appear inhibited or unnatural, others brash and overconfident, others will be their spontaneous selves and seem sensible, well informed and caring.

Voices which are rich and full of inflection will sound much better on the radio than a dry, reserved voice. Professional broadcasters are trained to put a lot of emphasis into their voices: '*Last night* an *armed* gunman *forced* his *way* into the *Bank of England* and *held four* staff *hostage*' –try it out on a tape recorder and you will see that it works. Regional accents can be a bonus providing they are not so strong as to make them hard to understand. They provide variety and interest, and should rarely be toned down. Women's voices can sometimes be a problem as, when forced to speak out, they can become hard and high-pitched, and middle-class accents have a tendency to come over as 'plummy' or strident. On the whole, the more natural and relaxed your voice is, the better it will sound.

There is a tendency in some voluntary organisations which do give radio or TV interviews fairly frequently for one person to become the 'media star'. This is all right up to a point, but there is no reason why it should always be the same person who appears, and it is always wise to have two or three people available so that you are not stuck when someone is away. It is also useful for someone to record an interview so that the person interviewed has a chance to listen to the result. This will help a lot in working out how you can improve your interview technique later on.

## What happens in an interview

Normally, whether the interview is live or pre-recorded, you will sit down with the interviewer who will discuss the scope of the interview. You have a right to ask what the first question will be, more than that kills spontaneity. The interviewer will also be checking that you can provide reasonable answers before you start recording or actually go 'on the air'.

The interviewer will normally 'take level' to test the equipment and balance the loudness of your voice. The microphone will normally be adjusted to your natural voice level, so try not to speak very quietly at this point and then start booming when the interview itself begins. The interviewer normally asks what you've had for breakfast. Don't just say 'nothing' and then shut up; he or she wants you to talk about *something*, regardless of what the subject is.

If the interview is in your office, the interviewer will also take simple precautions to improve acoustics, such as drawing curtains or blinds, shutting doors and windows, altering seating arrangements, and stopping telephones.

Going into the studio, especially to do a live interview, can be a nerve-racking experience. Flashing lights, large microphones, and the silence imposed on you when you are ushered into the live studio can all be very intimidating. Sometimes people will wave or make signals in the air at one another – including the person who is interviewing you in the middle of a sentence. These are usually cues as to what is happening next and nothing to do with you, so try not to become distracted.

You are usually given a very short space of time to get your piece across, and the time will seem even shorter than you expect. The space between 'And now we have Sally Rodgers of the Children's Care Association to explain the new proposals' and 'Sally Rodgers, thank you very much' will seem like the blinking of an eyelid so be ready to get the most out of it.

Overall, success in interviews is determined by your general approach. Be interesting. You are talking to one person. You want to inform, persuade, convince that person.

## Some general points about interviews

The interview is not, as some people might believe, a platform for you freely to express your views without interruption, nor is it a confrontation which either you or the interviewer must 'win'. The interviewer should ask the questions that he or she feels the listener would want to know, and also to an extent act as devil's advocate.

Beware of trying to get too many facts and figures into an interview. Listeners can't take them all in and tend to recall only *one* thing you said. The *overall impression* may count for more. There is also a temptation to say what you want to say, but then, because you are afraid of a silence, go on elaborating – and frequently muddling – what you just said. Don't do this. As soon as you stop the interviewer will ask the next question –a series of quick questions and answers will make a much better interview.

When being interviewed, you should not feel too restricted by the actual questions asked. Answer them, but make additional points and give examples where necessary or relevant. If you think you're being asked the wrong questions, then deflect them and get on to the point you want to make. You can easily say something like, 'That's a good point, but even more important is the fact that...' and then get across the point you really want to make. If you listen to the radio or watch TV interviews regularly you will see how often this ploy is used and how effective it is.

Similarly, if you are asked something you don't know, reply with something you *do* know. This gives the impression you do on the whole know what you're talking about. So, if you're asked, for example, what percentage of people are in particular need and you don't know, say something like 'I don't have the exact figures here with me -but it is a significant number and these people badly need our help if they are not to die of cold/lose benefits they are entitled to/etc.'

Do be absolutely clear what the message is that you want to get across. This may sound obvious, but it is surprising how often mistakes occur. For example, one local refugee action group had gone to do an interview on the local radio station, to launch a furniture appeal for Vietnamese refugees. Due to a misunderstanding between the group and the radio station, the reporter who interviewed a member of the group failed to mention exactly what they needed, and because a remark was made during the interview about the refugees 'finding the weather a bit chilly', the group's telephone was jammed with people offering the refugees winter clothes which they did not need or want.

Another obvious but vital point is to be properly briefed and prepared. When I was working in the press office of the Family Planning Association, I was once rung up at home early in the morning and asked to go straight into the BBC to do an interview on a new kind of contraceptive pill which had been made available. I didn't know much about this, but was told the information would be waiting for me at Broadcasting House to read before I did the interview. Needless to say it wasn't there when I arrived, and a researcher was waiting and panicking because I was scheduled to go on the air in just over five minutes! The material arrived and I had to skim through it in the lift on the way to the studio, still thinking there was a chance I could pull out. But before I knew what was happening I was in the studio with the green light on and a BBC voice saying, 'And here is Maggie Jones from the Family Planning Association to tell us about this new contraceptive pill...' Sounder liaison between the programme's presenter and the FPA press office would have avoided this panic.

Finally, if you want to get publicity, see it through -don't back out at the last minute. And just because you've been asked to do one interview, it doesn't mean you've become a star. To illustrate both these points, the chairman of one local voluntary group insisted his name went on the bottom of the press release. The local radio station rang up in the evening at home and asked him if he would come into the studio at 8.00 a.m. (peak listening time) to do an interview on the breakfast show. He rang the organisation complaining that this meant he had to get up at 6.30 a.m. and did he really have to go? When he was persuaded that he should, he was very annoyed that he was in and out in 10 minutes the following morning and that no one gave him a tour of the local radio station as he had expected.

## Training for broadcasting

A number of voluntary agencies offer training in how to use radio and television more effectively. These are listed in the appendix.

# 6
# Opportunities in Broadcasting

The broadcasting scene has changed considerably over the past ten years, with the expansion in local radio, the creation of Channel 4 television, the development of new systems such as teletext and Prestel, and the advent of satellite television. However, these are slight compared to the changes that we are likely to see over the next few years. The Broadcasting Act, which became law in November 1990, has started the process of increasing deregulation of the broadcast media, which may have far-reaching effects on the quality of future television, and on the documentary, educational and social action broadcasting which has been so useful in furthering the aims of voluntary organisations in the past.

Commercial television in the UK has been regulated through the Independent Broadcasting Authority, which granted licences to television companies and acted as a watchdog. The IBA is replaced by the Independent Television Commission, the ITC, which came into being on 1 January 1991. The ITC also takes over from the Cable Authority, and satellite television also comes under its remit. Control of commercial radio passes to the new Radio Authority.

New licences for television will be granted from 1993. Some of the existing independent television companies and some new ones have been awarded franchises. The ITC looked at what the TV company offered, and operated a 'quality threshold' in granting licences and looking for diversity in programming. However, when the new franchises are in operation the ITC will have lost the power to preview programmes and to approve schedules in advance. Self-regulation will be the order of the day. It does have a wide range of sanctions if the television company should renege on its promises, ranging from a warning letter, through fines to revocation of the licence if the TV company does not comply.

Although news, current affairs, religious and children's programmes must be provided, the Act does not list documentaries, educational and social action programmes as essential offerings by TV companies. The removal of such safeguards, and the increasing competition between a larger number of television channels, cable and satellite, with an inevitable drop in advertising revenue, mean that many voluntary organisations are afraid that the kind of programmes they believe in may not be made any more.

The situation will not really be clear until 1993 when the companies awarded new franchises start broadcasting, but voluntary groups have to some extent been reassured that the draft invitation to bid circulated by the ITC states that companies should include regional news and a wide range of material of local interest, including social action programmes.

A further potential threat to social action broadcasting is the clause which says that television programmes must reflect 'due impartiality'. Voluntary groups are afraid this may affect access programmes in which they want to make a strong argument which may be construed as 'political'. Formerly balance could be argued to be upheld across the range of programmes, so that an access programme could be seen to 'balance' the consensus view normally expressed in other programmes. The fact that a television company could be taken to court over a controversial programme is a serious threat to certain kinds of broadcasting.

The future of the BBC is also uncertain as wide-ranging reforms have been suggested. A possibility is that the TV licence will be removed and that the BBC will become a subscription service, with a possible decline in viewers. Many broadcasters and voluntary organisations are concerned that the old balance in broadcasting will go taking much of what is good and unique in British broadcasting with it. The existing 50-50 split between viewers of commercial TV and the BBC has done much to encourage competition and keep up standards.

For radio, the effects of deregulation may be even more far-reaching. There is now no limit on the amount of advertising allowed on commercial radio. The Radio Authority has issued codes covering advertising, sponsorship and programming, and radio stations will have to abide by these. The sanctions operated by the Authority are fines and taking back or shortening the radio station's licence. Radio stations will no longer be monitored and complaints will have to be made to the Authority.

Voluntary groups and broadcasters are all anxious about cuts in speech-based programmes, which are more expensive to make, in favour of music. However, there are more opportunities, too. There will be an expansion in local radio: the Radio Authority will be offering 27 licences for independent local radio stations, and 3 licences for national commercial radio stations, something that has not existed before. One will have to be speech-based, one non-pop and the third neither of these.

Until now, the broadcast media seem to have become increasingly aware of their involvement with the community and community action, and of the potential for achieving social action through broadcasting. On the whole, broadcasters themselves want to co-operate with voluntary groups. Despite the threat from increased competition and self-regulation, there are new opportunities opening up with a new TV channel –Channel 5 –cable and satellite, and local radio, which voluntary organisations can take advantage of.

NACAB, for example, is now running a 'CAB of the Air' on the BBC's new radio service, Radio 5, and Age Concern is applying for one of the new incremental radio licences to run a local radio station for the over 50s. Any voluntary organisation, whether small and local or large and national in scope, should be exploring new areas which are opening up and familiarising themselves with the opportunities available.

## Phone-ins and local radio

Many local radio stations have phone-ins; you can suggest a phone-in on the subject your organisation is concerned with and one of your members or staff, or a public figure known to you, to answer calls.

However, often the calls which you answer on air are the tip of the iceberg. Few calls can actually be dealt with on air in the allotted time, and some people, especially if the subject is a sensitive one, may want information or counselling in private. You may be able to arrange some back-up to deal with such calls, or give referral numbers which people can ring. In either case, there are likely to be a lot of calls which may be dealt with by the radio station staff during the programme, and afterwards there may be a lot of calls to your organisation from people who tried and failed to get through, who got through and were given your number, or were encouraged to ring after hearing the programme on their radio. Taking part in a two-hour phone-in may result in as much as two weeks' work for your organisation.

## Specialist programmes

There are a number of specialist programmes on both television and radio for minority audiences. These include programmes for the blind - such as Radio 4's weekly 'In Touch' programme –and for the deaf - e.g. Grampian's 'Sign Hear' or Radio 4's 'Does He Take Sugar?' for the handicapped, Central TV's 'Link', and Channel 4's 'Same Difference'. There are also special programmes for the elderly, the young unemployed, and for ethnic minorities –including such ventures as BBC Radio Leicester's '6.00 Show' with news, information, discussion and music for Asian listeners and Channel 4's Asian/Afro-Caribbean magazine programme 'Ebony'. 'Family Pride', a new Asian soap opera, Britain's first on TV, is being produced by Central Television. These programmes often have close links with the relevant voluntary organisations and can provide an excellent way of getting information across to a wide, yet specific, audience.

## The potential of documentaries and drama documentaries

A number of documentaries, drama documentaries and special 'social action' slots on television have brought particular areas of social concern home to a wider audience. Drama documentaries like 'Cathy Come Home' or documentaries like Yorkshire Television's 'Alice - A Fight for Life' have had enormous impact on the public and even on government policy making. In 1990 the drama-documentary

'Somewhere to Run' from Thames TV raised the question of young homeless people and worked closely with voluntary agencies dealing with this problem. Actors visited hostels to talk to young people and the agencies consulted suggested ideas and script changes. Some voluntary agencies have used soap operas as a way to raise issues. Some years ago the inclusion of a mentally handicapped Down's Syndrome child on 'Crossroads' brought this issue into the public eye, and resulted in money being raised for mental handicap charities from viewers together with offers of help. On 'Brookside' the problems of dyslexia were aired when Geoff Rogers' problems at school were traced to dyslexia. The effects of such publicity can be extraordinary. When East Enders Den and Angie went for marriage guidance counselling, Relate reported a 50 per cent increase in callers as a result. Radio programmes such as 'The Archers' regularly provide information on such matters as medical and social problems, safety on the roads and other issues where the giving of advice or information can be 'dressed up' in dramatic form.

How do you get your organisation's concerns into such programmes? The truth seems to be that so far, the initiative in making documentaries, 'drama docs' and bringing information on social issues into TV or radio 'soap opera' has come largely from the programme makers. A letter or telephone call out of the blue from a voluntary organisation wanting to get its message across is likely not to meet with too enthusiastic a response; however, it could be worth a try; you might hit lucky. The inclusion of the mentally handicapped child in 'Crossroads' came out of a follow-up meeting with MENCAP to ATV's documentary 'Silent Minority' about residents in long-stay mental handicap institutions.

More easy to get into are the regular 'social action' slots like Scottish Television's five-minute 'Action Line' or 'What's Your Problem?' (here subjects dealt with are often prompted by viewer's letters), the 'Thames Help' programme or ITV's network 'Link' programme for the disabled.

# Appeals

There are some regular appeals slots on radio and television such as BBC Radio 4's 'The week's good cause'. Appeals advisory committees advise on which organisations should be allocated space from those which have applied. The Central Appeals Advisory Committee advises for England and there are separate committees for Northern Ireland, Scotland and Wales.

In addition to choosing between applicants for the regular appeals slots on ITV and BBC television and national radio, the committees advise on some special annual appeals, e.g. the BBC Children in Need appeal and the Wireless for the Blind appeal. Other special appeals slots are decided on by the broadcasters in much the same way as a theme might be chosen for a documentary. Recently television appeals have become larger and more sophisticated, following the first spectacular fund-raising 'telethon' on Thames TV in 1980. In 1988 the entire ITV network combined for the first time to broadcast a live entertainment marathon to raise money for charity. Telethon 88 raised money for a number of charities with different priorities. Every ITV company now has its own Telethon Office and Trust to advise on where the money goes.

Normally, the organisation on behalf of whom the appeal is made is not involved directly, and its address and telephone number is not given; money is sent in to the radio or TV station to be passed on. Interestingly, some organisations have found that just as much money is raised from a documentary on a particular issue as from a direct appeal, so if you fail to get an appeal slot, it could be worth trying to interest broadcasters in making a documentary.

# 'Access' programmes

The term 'access' was first applied to broadcasting in the early 1970s and meant that people other than professionals should have 'access' to making radio and television programmes, which would not be controlled by the producers and editors. The BBC's 'Open Door' – which came to the end of its run in March 1983 –was Britain's first and longest-running networked television access programme. Would-be programme-makers – either groups or individuals – could fill in an application to make an Open Door and the BBC's Community Programme Unit (CPU), together with a team of outside observers, would then select applicants. 'Grapevine' and 'Something Else' were also made as access programmes, through in different ways. 'Grapevine' gave sympathetic coverage to self-help and community action initiatives, while 'Something Else' programmes were made by groups of young people.

The 'Open Door' slot has been replaced by 'Open Space', a new series subtitled 'Where the public sets the agenda'. The programmes will vary from those where groups produce the whole programme, to those where the CPU make the programmes based on ideas sent in by people who do not themselves have the time or resources to go in for actual programme-making. The CPU, however, will still in effect be 'setting the agenda' to the extent that it will give priority to programmes covering issues which are not usually addressed in broadcasting, or which seem to be habitually distorted.

Channel 4 has also paid attention to the need for more 'access' type programmes, and has encouraged independent producers to make programmes addressing issues not usually covered on television, and to provide programmes for audiences which have been poorly catered for in the past. Channel 4 has access slots such as 'Right to Reply' presented by Brian Hayes. A new access programme, 'Free for All' started in 1991.

There have been some problems with access programmes. Some groups, when invited to make a programme, felt dissatisfied that they were not offered the same kinds of sets and back-up as used for a prestige programme like, for example, 'Panorama'. Others thought that the professionalism of the broadcasters, who want to produce a certain 'standard of programme', clashed with the groups making the programme, who feel they have an urgent message to deliver.

## Teletext, Oracle and Ceefax

Oracle (ITV) and Ceefax (BBC) are the two systems – both called 'teletext' – by which specifically adapted television sets can receive pages of news and information on their television screens. The user can call up the relevant pages at will with a hand-held 'key'. Once the set has been 'converted' there are no more charges (the service is paid for by the licence fee or advertising). Both Oracle and Ceefax can also be used over a normal TV picture, and by this means both networks now offer subtitling on a number of popular programmes to assist the hard of hearing. Teletext is also used to subtitle programmes for the deaf and hard of hearing. The 1990 Broadcasting Act gives a commitment to increase sub-titling on commercial television to 50 per cent of programmes within five years, and Channel 5 will have subtitling from its launch.

There is also some potential for voluntary organisations to run programmes on Ceefax and Oracle. In September 1980, The Volunteer Centre provided the first 'programme' of information on volunteering. The material was converted to six stories, or frames, which were broadcast for a week and have since been replaced with new frames every Friday.

Voluntary organisations which have news likely to be of national interest can send press releases to Ceefax and Oracle for inclusion on their regular and constantly updated news pages, just as they would to any other newspaper or news agency.

Teletext can also link in with broadcast programmes, providing further information about voluntary organisations that have taken part in programmes. So if you know that a BBC or ITV programme is going to feature your organisation, why not approach Ceefax or Oracle and ask them to include some back-up information?

CEEFAX
*Magazine and news items:* Copy Taster, CEEFAX, Room 7059, BBC Television Centre, Wood Lane, London W12 7RJ.

ORACLE
*Magazine items:* ORACLE, London Weekend Television, South Bank Television Centre, Kent House, London SE1 9LT.
*News items:* Editor, ORACLE, ITN House, 48 Wells Street, London W1P 4DE.

## Prestel

In essence, Prestel is an electronic information service provided through a TV set connected by telephone to a computer. It is different from Ceefax and Oracle in that the information is provided by independent companies, not the TV companies, and because the viewer with a set adapted to receive Prestel can, at the press of a button, summon up 'pages' of information on the television screen. Viewers pay British Telecom for the telephone and computer time they have used in their quarterly telephone bill, and pay charges for some 'pages' of information (but not others). You can also 'respond' and pay for an item like a plane ticket with your credit card. In principle, viewers could also let a voluntary organisation know that they want to volunteer.

Various attempts have been made to make the Prestel system available to voluntary organisations. In its early days, some voluntary organisations were offered free pages of information to put into the system. However, when the three-month trial period was over and voluntary organisations were asked to pay -a charge of between £1,000 and £4,000 a year plus £1 to £4 to rent a frame -most considered that not enough ordinary domestic consumers were using Prestel to make it worth while.

So far, Prestel has not been popular with the consumer, partly because of the expense and partly because the system is constantly changing to attract custom and as technology develops. The development of cable television means that Prestel may become available through cable rather than down the telephone, and link-up systems already exist with home computers. However, as Prestel and other videotext systems become cheaper and more popular, they may well provide voluntary organisations with an effective means of getting information across to people in their own homes.

## Satellite television

Satellite television was finally launched in Britain in February 1989 with the start of Sky Television. British Satellite Broadcasting, BSB, followed in 1990, but was only to last a few months before merging with Sky to form British Sky Broadcasting, offering a mixture of the Sky Channels broadcast on the Astra satellite and the BSB channels on Marco Polo. However, the IBA ruled that the takeover was illegal and have withdrawn the franchise to broadcast from the Marco Polo satellite, leaving Sky with two movie channels, one sport, one entertainment, and one news. In 1990 Sky television was reaching 1.4 million homes.

The Astra satellite can receive 16 channels - seven of them English-language, and the rest other European channels. Subscribers pay extra to decode some channels. While most satellite channels are news, sport or pure entertainment, some channels do offer opportunities for voluntary organisations. The Children's Channel, for instance, carries a range of educational programmes, and 25 per cent of the programmes they broadcast are made in-house, including children's drama. Recently the Pre-school Playgroups Association have worked on programmes for playgroups to be broadcast on the Children's Channel. Lifestyle, a channel aimed at women, has drama and discussions on health, family and other matters.

There are potential opportunities offered by satellite technology, such as development in educational broadcasting launched on the Olympus satellite in 1989. A co-operative association of users called Eurostep including schools, colleges, cultural and professional organisations, co-ordinates nine hours a day of experimental educational programmes on a broad range of subjects and levels of attainment.

## Cable television

After a long period in which people were reluctant to invest in cable television in Britain, cable finally took off in 1990. The Cable Authority has granted 135 franchises, which will merge with the IBA to form the ITC in 1991. At the end of 1990 only 26 cable companies were actually operating; just over 371,000 households were connected to cable. Most of the investment in cable has come from the US and Canada; over 90 per cent of cable companies in Britain will be American-owned.

The services offered on cable vary from company to company. All will offer the satellite channels, entertainment channels, and videotape-delivered programmes. Almost all cable operators will offer local programming and programming for ethnic minorities, the deaf, and so on; this will be a legal requirement for franchises granted after the 1990 Broadcasting Act. Subscribers to cable can choose the number of channels they wish to subscribe to.

Cable offers other possibilities. The modern broadband cable used can carry as many as 40 channels and can send signals as well as receive them. Cable can be used to do home shopping, banking, and operate security alarms. Four cable operators already offer such services. In a few areas cable is also used to link hospitals for teaching, and operates within schools. Cable can also be used as an alternative phone network.

Cable television will be funded both by advertising and by subscription. Research carried out by the Institute of Local Television shows that people are interested in local news and programming. A survey in Edinburgh in 1990 showed that 83 per cent of the sample were willing to pay a monthly subscription for 'a quality local television service with an emphasis on local news'. In the US and Germany, open-access channels enable people to make their own programmes for television, and some people look forward to an age of 'TV literacy' where people will be able to make their own television directly rather than using professionals as mediators.

Some voluntary organisations have expressed concern that the cable operators are unlikely to be interested in social action broadcasting, although they might build such possibilities into their planned programmes in a cynical bid to win franchises, and then drop these programmes if they appear poorly produced or unpopular. A further problem is that if audiences turn largely to viewing cable, then the existing TV channels may come under increasing pressure to compete with cable companies for advertising and drop social action slots in favour of programmes with higher viewing rates.

# Video

Video recorders are now in use in nearly 60 per cent of British homes, and many households belong to video libraries. Voluntary organisations could make much more use of video as an alternative to television programmes –making information videos which people can borrow, buy or hire. If a TV programme is made with a voluntary organisation, it could consider keeping the non-theatrical rights so that they can use the video for educational purposes.

# 7
# Community Service Announcements

In recent years a new opportunity has opened up for voluntary organisations to get their message across, by using the community service announcements offered through the ITV regional companies and through local radio, both BBC and independent.

A community service announcement is a short –often 30 second – 'advertisement' by a voluntary organisation, which is broadcast in the breaks between or during programmes. On local radio they have a variety of different names –community information slots, action lines, community service announcements are a few.

Many local radio stations, and 12 of the 16 regional ITV stations, offer some kind of community service announcement scheme, apart from the similar slots 'Thames Help' and LWT's 'The Day', and it's worth approaching them to find out what they offer and how your organisation can be considered for a slot.

Public service announcements are free. Whether produced on local radio or regional television, they are all subject to certain standards and controls: you cannot necessary just record your own tape or video and have it put out over the air. Local radio stations very enormously in the amount of support and expertise that will be given to producing a PSA. Some radio stations will just record a straight read-out of a script that they have agreed with you. Others will take a more imaginative approach, perhaps incorporating sound-effects or music.

For television, PSAs are covered by guidelines originally drawn up by the Independent Broadcasting Authority (IBA), now the Independent Television Commission (ITC). These stipulate that all PSAs have to be identified as such on the screen so that they are not confused by the viewer with ordinary paid commercials. PSAs cannot be used for fund-raising, or for political or religious purposes, and they have to be approved by the local ITC regional officer before they are broadcast. Until the end of 1992 the ITC will be continuing to operate much as the IBA has in the past; the guidelines on PSAs will continue to exist. From 1993 when the new franchises are granted for Channel 3 companies, the situation will be rather different.

With all PSAs, the onus is on the voluntary organisation to get in touch with the radio or TV station. For radio the approach can be more informal – over the telephone or by personal contact. With television an application has to go either direct to the television station, or, with some schemes, through local voluntary or statutory bodies which administer it. Each application is normally assessed in terms of local needs, the organisation's ability to deal with the response, and whether it satisfies the ITC guidelines. For radio, different stations allow different kinds of PSAs: some may allow fund raising, others only appeals for volunteers and advertising of services.

Once an application for a television PSA has been accepted, the organisation and the television station will get together for a session where the PSA script is finalised and recorded. Some PSAs consist only of a representative from the organisation reading the PSA script, others have a presentation with commentary and background slides, production illustrations and so on. Some have specially produced film, involving scriptwriters and actors.

The PSA then has to be approved by the local ITC regional officers and scheduled for transmission by the television company. Most PSAs are transmitted for only one week, usually being screened about five times in that week. The facilities and size of budget available for making public service announcements very quite widely from region to region, although within any given region voluntary organisations should all receive the same treatment.

Many of the same points will apply to scripting a PSA for radio. The better the script you submit, the more enthusiastic the response you are likely to get from the station and, of course, from the listener. If possible, use short punchy sentences when scripting a PSA, keeping the language informal (refer to the listener directly as 'you' for impact). A PSA of 30-45 seconds is only 90 to 120 words read out, so the message will have to very brief. You can practice reading out such scripts on a tape recorder and see how they come over, and try out different approaches before you contact the radio station to take things a stage further. If you are not sure of how to do the script, or what potential there is for using different voices or sound effects, then some radio stations will help prepare a suitable script for you, providing you are clear about the points you want to get across.

## How do you deal with the response?

As important, however, as getting to do a PSA in the first place is what you are going to do with the response that is generated. There is no point in going on the air to do a PSA to appeal for volunteers if you are not going to be able to answer enquiries or provide work for them when they ring up, or to provide enough services to people who have seen them 'advertised'.

At the end of each PSA you must give information about where viewers can find out more or get the services they want. This can be the address of the voluntary organisation concerned, its phone number, a central telephone number provided by the television company or radio station, a PO Box number or any combination of these. Clearly, if you give a telephone number that people can ring immediately after the PSA has ended, this is likely to elicit a greater response then asking people to write in. But there is no point in going for this option if you only have one telephone line or if you won't be able to find enough people to answer the telephones, or if the office is not open on Saturdays, Sundays and evenings when the PSA is likely to be broadcast.

The arrangements for dealing with the response to a PSA should have been worked out in advance of the broadcast being made. It should form part of your application, especially for a television PSA.

Another problem, especially with television companies which broadcast over a wide area, is that the PSA may be watched by people outside your immediate area so that some potential clients or volunteers who contact you may have to be redirected to other organisations or services nearer to their homes.

# What kind of response can you expect?

The response differs enormously according to the kind of message and service that is being broadcasted. A recent report showed that on television, small local appeals usually produce 20 to 40 replies, and regional broadcasts around 60 to 130 replies. In its first three years the ATV/Central Independent Television PSA scheme helped 116 organisations find almost 13,000 new clients, while another 148 organisations attracted over 9,000 new volunteers.

Occasionally, TV PSAs will generate a very large response. An appeal for the Samaritans, broadcast on LWT seeking volunteers in and around London, generated over 800 potential volunteers. A PSA for Television South promoting Gingerbread holidays for single parents had a response from over 900 viewers.

For some PSAs, however, the response cannot be judged solely by the number of people who contact the organisation. Many more viewers and listeners will have had their attention drawn to the problems of handicapped people or to the need to use birth control, for example, and act on this information at a later stage.

Some of the issues involved in producing a PSA on television are brought out in the following account by Romie Goodchild, former press officer at the Family Planning Association.

A community information announcement encouraging teenage boys to take more responsibility for birth control was shown seven times on ITV in the London region over the weekend 9-11 December 1983. It was the first time that a birth control message had been allowed on British television.

The 30 second announcement was produced by London Weekend Television's Community Information Service for the Family Planning Association and Brook Advisory Centres.

The announcement was originally planned to be shown in January 1983, but the Independent Broadcasting Authority was concerned about the script and asked for it to be amended. The IBA continued to insist that the announcement should be shown after 9.00 p.m. It was in fact shown three times on Friday night/Saturday morning starting at 10.40 p.m. and four times in the early hours of Sunday morning starting at 00.30 a.m. The film featured two teenagers, played by actors, having a conversation in a hamburger bar about a friend who has 'got a girl into trouble'. Adam Faith then advised teenagers 'If you want to find out more about birth control or just talk to someone, ring 928-5656 now and they'll tell you where young people are welcome.'

The FPA organised for telephones, provided by LWT, to be manned by volunteers from the FPA and Brook who would be able to offer information and advice on services and contraception generally. The volunteers were provided with lists of clinics in the London area where young people could attend, other referral information and leaflets. There were a total of 354 calls (197 on Friday/Saturday and 157 on Sunday morning). The smaller number on Sunday morning would probably be explained by the lateness of the showing.

The calls came almost entirely from young people –the target audience – and predominantly from young men (three quarters were male and one quarter female). Around a quarter of the callers asked for advice or information about services and methods. A high proportion of the young men, two out of every five, lost confidence and rang off. Several callers (one in ten) took the opportunity to call about other worries such as sexual problems, sexually transmitted diseases and difficulties in relationships.

There was very little opposition to the message –three calls in all, whereas eight callers expressed support. One of these, a teacher, expressed her delight at finding a source of information to use in sex education work which she regarded as necessary at her school. Another, a parent of teenagers, expressed the view that the showings were far too late.

Those who took part felt that the phone-in had been worthwhile and provided some young men with information they would not otherwise have received.

When in June 1984 the same PSA was shown at 9.00, 9.30, 10.00 and 11.00 p.m. on a Friday evening, nearly 400 calls were received. There was not one call of complaint.

Dealing with the response generated by a PSA or any other TV appeal can involve an enormous amount of preparation and follow-up. As an illustration of how much work can be involved, the following account, condensed from a report by Liz Dickie of Contact, shows the experience of the organisation Contact when it was featured on a five-minute appeal on the 'Thames Help' programme.

Contact is a voluntary scheme operating nationally to provide companionship for elderly people who live alone and who, because they cannot get out without help, are becoming isolated and lonely. They are introduced to a Contact group of volunteers and other elderly people and meet regularly once a month for Sunday afternoon tea in the home of a volunteer host. Long waiting lists of elderly people in need of friendship in London prompted an approach by Contact to the 'Thames Help' programme.

Considerable organisation went into arranging the selection of a Contact group to be filmed, the venue and the timing. A check-list of questions covering the filming was prepared by Contact and systematically worked through with the producer and director on a visit to the home of the volunteer host who was providing her home for the filming.

The film was to show a Contact group in action. The presenter joined the group for the afternoon, talking to the old people and her conversations with them were filmed. A very brief script was prepared in which a three-sentence appeal for volunteer drivers would be made. This script was agreed with Contact before the appeal went out.

Contact had ten days' notice of the date of transmission. In that time they informed all their group leaders, hosts, donors, selected journalists, social workers and agencies who referred elderly people to them and volunteer bureaux organisers in the Thames Valley area. National advertising was adjusted to alert readers to the appeal.

'Thames Help' advised Contact to anticipate up to 500 responses. Dealing with this necessitated planning the mailings before transmission and recruiting help from among Contact's experienced volunteer group leaders to take the calls and later to assist in preparing and briefing potential new volunteers.

Thirty Contact group leaders and volunteers were briefed to man the telephones at Thames Television and in the three hours following the programme at 6.40 p.m. they took 601 telephone calls. A 1.20 p.m. repeat produced a further 90 calls and during the following week 14 calls to Contact's office. Of the 705 callers, seven were from elderly people asking for help.

The caller's name, address and daytime telephone number were recorded on a two-part form (one for Contact, one for Thames). A second team of volunteers addressed envelopes and filled them with a letter from the presenter and a 'Help' booklet about volunteering.

When this was completed, the forms were separated and batched alphabetically. Because Contact wanted to approach callers with an invitation to a new members' evening in their area or refer them direct to a group leader of a group with a vacancy, they decided to analyse and batch the response before mailing out information about Contact. Sorting the 705 responses by London borough and county proved the most time-consuming and exhausting part of the whole exercise. It took three people eight days. An alphabetical card index was compiled by one volunteer (three evenings' work) and was used to record the response from the volunteer, the follow-up by the office and the ultimate result. It also helped if volunteers phoned to claim they had 'heard nothing more'.

Various problems did arise. Inevitably names had been misspelt when they were taken down; some detective work was needed to track down Mrs Spellman whose name had been transcribed as Miss Feltham. Other names and addresses were equally incorrect.

A series of new members' evenings were held to introduce and brief new members. Some six weeks after the appeal, 120 volunteers had been placed in Contact groups and in the seven months which followed, 14 new Contact groups were started.

As a result of the appeal, a further 184 elderly people were part of a Contact group. This was achieved by hours of evening and weekend work. No greater take-up has been obtained by any other method of recruiting volunteers and none produced the volume of response achieved by the 'Thames Help' programme.

# 8
# Dealing with Hostile Publicity

No guide to how to use the media would be complete without looking at the other side of the coin –when the media uses you, exaggerating, making false claims and misrepresenting your case to make a 'good story'. All publicity is not good publicity, especially for a voluntary organisation whose funding might be affected, whether it be government money or private donations.

To a certain extent many voluntary organisations trade on the goodwill extended to groups who are obviously trying to do useful work. However, this is not always the case; some of the public at large, and many cynical journalists, are suspicious of any 'do-gooding' and are always delighted to find examples of charities that appear to be making a surplus (rather than spending all the money donated to them) or misusing their funds. Journalists are always on the look-out for such stories and will pursue them when they can.

Another problem is that the good work a voluntary organisation does over the years is seldom considered 'news', though you may get good coverage for something like the 25th or 50th anniversary of an established charity, especially if it has become a household name. But the moment such an organisation puts a foot wrong –or appears to have done so –there is a rush of bad publicity. For example, in early 1984 Oxfam received wide coverage for its 40th anniversary, including a full-page report in *The Times*. However, it also received some bad publicity when one national newspaper 'discovered' that an ex-member of a guerilla organisation in a Third World country had been given Oxfam training for a development project. So Oxfam found itself the butt of headlines like 'Third World Charity Funds Guerillas'.

## Unpopular causes

While some voluntary organisations are seen as basically 'good causes' by the media – for example, those helping the handicapped, maltreated children, or alleviating poverty in developing countries – there are some which represent unpopular issues. These will find themselves the focus of constant harassment, misquoting and misrepresentation by the press. Indeed, these organisations will have to have a very different approach to press work: for them, dealing with the media does not constitute seeking publicity and putting out press releases so much as fending off journalists and correcting misinformation. Their success may indeed be judged not so much by what *does* get into the press as by what is kept out.

Organisations which often receive hostile publicity include those asserting the rights of ethnic minority groups, women, and gay people ; those who represent freedom of choice in life or death issues such as euthanasia or abortion; those who appear to be identified with political parties or other organisations seeking to bring about radical social change. All voluntary organisations may stray into this category at some time or another; the public may be happy to help handicapped people but resent it if handicapped people actually demonstrate that they should have equal rights to employment; people may feel sympathetic to the problems of being in a one-parent family but resent it if single parents campaign for greater benefits.

There is a danger, however, in believing that what appears in the media inevitably reflects the views of 'the public at large'. Members of the general public are often more sympathetic to 'unpopular' causes than the media. Anna Durrell of the Campaign for Homosexual Equality believes that there are considerable pitfalls in thinking that what appears in the media will either reflect or influence what most people think. For example, according to Home Office/Gallup polls, 75 per cent of people think that there should be no discrimination against gay people –something you would never imagine from media coverage of homosexuality.

The press have certain stock tactics when they want to discredit a particular cause. They exaggerate and distort what the organisation is saying –for example, presenting supporters of voluntary euthanasia as actually wanting it to be compulsory. In these instances, issuing a press release denial is not likely to result in much publicity; a better approach is to write a letter to the newspaper stating your real views and policies. There is more chance that a letter will be published, and the letters column is often as widely and carefully read as the news pages.

Representatives of such groups soon develop skills in how to deflect the enemy. First of all, it is very important that any group whose cause is likely to be unpopular with the media should have very clear and carefully worded policies on issues which are likely to be controversial, so that these can be quoted promptly and succinctly to the press when needed. A standard journalistic tack is to phone up and say, 'We understand that your policy is such-and-such. Is that true?' On some occasions to say 'yes' or 'no' is equally damning. What you need to be able to do is give your own policy in your own words and say that this has been agreed by your committee and is written in your last annual report or publicity leaflet. This makes it more difficult for the journalist to misrepresent you.

You can also turn the policies into press statements ready to send out. When issuing a press release or statement, you have to make sure it is very brief and that no part of it can be quoted out of context. You also have to guess what the reaction to your activities will be, and to pick up any embarrassing events before they happen and try to pre-empt them, to undermine the journalist's story. If you know what a certain event or decision that you have made will result in bad publicity, then it can help to put across your side of the story first, rather than say nothing and wait in hope that it won't be picked up. Sometimes, however, it may result in stirring up bad publicity by drawing attention to the issue.

It is usually a mistake to issue a denial of a general slur on 'pro-abortion groups' or 'race relations organisations' and the like. This can be counter-productive, as not only will they almost certainly be ignored, but worse, your organisation's name may be knocked around more specifically in relation to that issue: people will assume that because you protested, it must have been you that was meant and you must have something to be worried about.

One example of this was of the organisation Gingerbread, which campaigns and provides support for single-parent families. A story appeared in one local paper about an 'orgy' which allegedly had been held by a local group called Gingerbread. In fact, this group was not affiliated to Gingerbread at all (and had simply held a rather wild party). However, a number of local Gingerbread groups immediately rang up and wrote letters to their local papers protesting that they were very respectable indeed, all of which led to much more publicity than the original article, and led many readers to assume that the offending group *was* a genuine member of Gingerbread.

If you protest too often in such circumstances it may mean being ignored when you really *do* need to make a denial, i.e. where you have had a policy attributed specifically to you which you do not hold. Here, a speedy denial or letter to the editor is essential.

However, there are some positive things that you can do to use the media. The first of these is to make sure that there is always a telephone number for journalists to ring where they can be sure of speaking to someone to check a point. Most journalists will do this if it is made easy for them, and it can make a lot of difference. This is one area where building up a personal relationship with journalists pays dividends.

In promoting a cause, figures are very useful –for instance results of research, or opinion polls which show greater public support for an issue than expected. Also, outstanding examples of need, discrimination or suffering can be useful publicity; people will often be sympathetic to individual cases where they might disapprove of something in the abstract.

Another thing you can do if you're promoting an unpopular cause is to find a sympathetic freelance journalist, feature writer, TV or radio researcher or producer, and get them to put forward a sympathetic idea. An extensive, one-off article or programme reflecting what your organisation is really about will go a lot further than endlessly issuing press releases, most of which fall on deaf ears and are unused.

# Avoiding hostile publicity

Almost any voluntary organisation may find itself the recipient of bad publicity. The chances of damaging coverage will be increased if there is any possibility of suspicion that you are wasting money; duplicating effort; not practising what you preach; or subject to internal disputes and divisions. Obviously, the better your organisation's general image, the less vulnerable you will be. The way the annual report and accounts are presented, the manner in which the organisation answers its telephones and deals with enquiries, and the way that it makes its achievements known are all important. If you don't present yourself well, people may assume that you're not doing anything, or are doing it badly.

Voluntary organisations, especially small ones, sometimes lack a certain professionalism in their management and organisational structures. This can lead to poor decisions being taken about such matters as buying, selling or renting property, employing the right staff; assessing priorities; and presenting their work to the public. All these things can lead to press accusations that a voluntary organisation is wasting its resources either accidentally or, sometimes, even deliberately. Every few months the details of some unfortunate move by a voluntary organisation are reported in the press.

Of most interest of all to journalists, however, are the internal divisions and disputes which seem to affect voluntary groups where people care deeply about the causes they are promoting. Clashes between committees of volunteers and staff are also frequent, but if serious enough to affect the organisation's work, can be of great interest to the media.

Some examples of voluntary organisations which received a lot of publicity over internal disputes include Shelter in 1973 when its director was sacked; MIND in 1981 when its director resigned over cuts in the charity's spending; and Task Force (now Pensioners Link), when the organisation was nearly closed down by the management board when they and the staff were in dispute. Amnesty International's British Section also received a lot of publicity after a reorganisation plan split the staff and led to the dismissal of its director. A second wave of publicity came a year or so later in a dispute between staff and management over the appointment of a new director.

More recent examples which resulted in newspaper articles involved the sacking by the London Lighthouse (which runs a residential centre and hospice for those terminally ill with AIDS) of a worker on probation who had AIDS, because he was two weeks behind with his work. This clearly undermined the caring image the charity was seeking to get across. Eight original managers had been sacked, paid off, or resigned due to disputes with the director. The Vegetarian Society also received bad publicity in 1991 when four members accused the society of electoral irregularities and of misleading and potentially illegal accounting procedures. At the same time the Parkinson's Disease Society admitted that elections to its council of management had been rigged, and that up to 2,000 ballot papers were forged during elections in 1990.

Apart from damage wrought internally by such disputes, the fact of their becoming public can erode the confidence of both donors and clients. If such disputes do occur, the press officer, or those who normally speak to the press, can find themselves in the invidious position of having to speak for an organisation which no longer has one view; he or she may feel forced to take sides. Obviously the most damaging thing is for everyone within the organisation to run to the press and 'tell all' at every stage of the dispute. However, a press officer who tries to cover up or merely presents the 'official' point of view may not help either, but merely fuel a journalist's interest in the story.

It is probably best to take the line that 'Yes, we do have a conflict, but both sides are discussing how to resolve it and we will issue a statement when the conflict is resolved.' Obviously, individuals within an organisation with different points of view should not argue their views publicly through the media.

Despite the disadvantages of this sort of publicity, which is outside the organisation's planning and control and can be very dangerous, there is sometimes a positive spin-off. Some organisations find they have never had so much publicity, and that knowledge of the organisation and its work gets across to a wider audience, as with the Task Force dispute. Sometimes the impression that is left behind is that of members of a voluntary organisation struggling to do its work against all the odds.

# How to complain to the press

Some hostile publicity will be completely unjustified, and the reports which appear are distorted or untrue. What can a voluntary organisation do if it has been misquoted or misrepresented in the press, on radio or on television?

The answer is –complain. Your main objective will be to have the misleading report corrected so that the public will not be left with the wrong impression. A secondary objective, however, and one which may be as important in the long run, is to see that the same kind of mistake – or deliberate misrepresentation – does not happen again. Journalists usually work fast and on one or two stories at the same time, and sometimes at second or third hand, so it is easy for mistakes to be made. If you don't let journalists know they have got something wrong, they will nearly always think that they have got it right.

With newspapers, radio or TV you should write or telephone immediately, pointing out the factual error. Most national newspapers have ombudsmen whose job it is to rule on complaints, and to issue reprimands where necessary. For TV, there is a duty officer who will log your complaint; follow this up with a letter. You should send one letter to the journalist or radio/TV programme involved and another to the editor of the paper or the head of the radio/TV station. Complaints are usually followed up internally even if you get no more than a brief apology.

Do not mix up factual errors with charges of bias or prejudice. Factual errors are much easier to deal with, and so are obvious examples of misrepresentation, but charges of bias are very hard to prove. Journalists are used to being accused of bias, often from both sides at the same time, and tend to shrug it off.

Sometimes accusations of bias *will* bear fruit. One voluntary group was interviewed on a local radio station, and their representative's words were cut up in the edited interview and interspersed with 'she said' and 'she claimed' in such a way as to make it look as if she were actually lying. When this was taken up with the head of the radio station, an apology was given and the journalist concerned reprimanded.

If a newspaper or radio/TV programme has got something badly wrong, they will usually do something to rectify it. Even if they are clearly in the wrong, they will resist printing or broadcasting a correction and in any case, would rarely give it the same prominence. They may print a letter pointing out the facts, and this is valuable, because letters are widely read. They may mention the true facts in a follow-up piece, or say something like 'It has now been made clear that the real figure of ... was x per cent, not the y per cent quoted in yesterday's report', though this is unusual. Sometimes an offer will be made to run a feature or broadcast a programme at a later date that sets the record straight or shows your organisation in a better light, if it is obvious a mistake has been made.

If you have a complaint about a broadcast programme, it is usually more constructive to complain in writing to an official at the top, with a copy to the editor of the programme concerned, as mentioned above. It is also worth trying such programmes as Channel 4's 'Right to Reply'. There are official bodies to whom you can complain, however. The IBA's role in regulating broadcasting has been taken over by the Broadcasting Standards Council as the new Independent Television Council (ITC) has a reduced regulatory role. The Broadcasting Standards Council will handle complaints from the public about the screen portrayal of violence, sex, and standards of taste and decency. The Broadcasting Complaints Commission handles complaints of unjust or unfair treatment and allegations of unwarranted invasion of privacy in radio, television, cable and satellite. It is a statutory body and often adjudicates in cases where companies or professional bodies dispute the way they have been portrayed.

For newspapers there is the Press Complaints Commission (PCC), which took over from the old Press Council in January 1991. The PCC has drawn up a new code of practice for journalists based on the old Press Council code and the recommendations of the Calcutt Committee, whose 1990 report on newspaper misbehaviour was responsible for the setting up of the new commission. Although, like the Press Council, the PCC will have no 'teeth', it is believed by many to be preferable to the alternative statutory controls over newspapers. The PCC is largely funded by the press, and the majority of the committee are representatives of the newspaper industry, so its claims to be impartial will be met with scepticism by many. The PCC accepts complaints from anyone who feels they have been abused or misrepresented by the press, or, at its discretion, from people concerned about ethical standards or practices.

If there is a serious misrepresentation of your organisation or its work, another option is to threaten a libel action. By law, only individuals - not organisations - can be victims of libel. However, if an organisation is said to be involved in corrupt practices, then the management committee or director could sue for libel, arguing that by implication they are being accused personally. However, there is little point in taking such an action unless you have the money to back it up. Libel cases are notoriously expensive and the judgements are notoriously uncertain. However, this applies to both sides, so a sharp letter from a solicitor may produce a retraction.

# 9
# In Conclusion

The purpose of this practical guide has been to show you how you can make the most of your own resources to use the media. If you follow the information given here and take time and trouble to build up your relations with the media, you should find that the publicity you get will help achieve your aims and get your message across to a wider audience, both of potential clients and decision makers. Doing it yourself is the key to this success.

Many voluntary organisations without the resources to pay an experienced press officer to carry out press work, or without enough of the right sort of work to make this worthwhile, are tempted to employ outside agencies - to do press work for them where necessary. The idea is that these people will have all the necessary information about press contacts, how to send out a press release, and how to word it in a way the press will like, and that you will be paying a fee only when and where you need publicity.

While there are occasions where this can work well, on the whole, the use of PR agencies is not to be recommended. For a start, the PR agency can never know all the ins and outs of your work, or perhaps be sensitive to attitudes which you hold which may not seem relevant at first to the issue in hand. So while the agency may be able to produce and mail out a competent press release, when journalists telephone for further information, the agency may be unable to provide it or any additional details about your organisation and its work. PR agencies have even been known to provide misleading information.

In addition, many PR agencies will appoint a particular person to a task to deal with one client; if that person is not available, then no one at the agency may know anything about it, in which case the journalist may be left at a loose end. For example, one PR agency which had written and put out a press release for a voluntary organisation had put no reference to the organisation's address or telephone number, giving only the agency's number. The person at the agency responsible for the release was on holiday that week, and no one else there had the voluntary body's address for the journalist to get in touch.

In the long term, using a PR agency is liable to prove more expensive than doing the work yourself. Though it may save time and trouble in the short run, there is no real substitute for building up your own direct relationship with the press and other media. A PR agency is unlikely to have the same enthusiasm, interest in and knowledge of your cause which will stir up support and interest journalists in your stories, and in any case, journalists usually prefer to deal directly with the organisation they are writing about.

In conclusion, then, using the media successfully involves a great deal more than simply sending out occasional press releases and hoping for the best, or relying on an outside agency to do this for you. It involves organising internal structures so that you can communicate effectively with the press and broadcast media; working at a local level to cultivate the local press, radio and other media; making contact with a wide range of media representatives and feeding in ideas; careful forethought and planning of any press campaign, conference, or media event; and longer-term future planning to exploit the new areas of opportunity which the media offer as they open up. If you do this well, then you should get a lot more out of the media for your organisation than Andy Warhol's ephemeral 15 minutes of fame.

# Appendix 1
# Useful Addresses

*Broadcasting Consortium*
c/o NCVO
26 Bedford Square
London WC1B 3HU
Tel. 071-636 7866
Fax 071-436 3188
The National Council for Voluntary Organisations undertakes policy work on broadcasting and supports the activities of the Broadcasting Consortium. This is a coalition of national charities who are working to protect and enlarge voluntary organisations' access to radio and TV. The consortium welcomes new members who want to get involved in their work.

*Broacasting Support Services*
252 Western Avenue
London W3 6XJ
Tel. 081-992 5522
Fax 081-993 6281
A charity which runs helplines and provides follow-up services for viewers and listeners on BBC, Channel 4, ITV and other media.

*Community Radio Association*
119 Southbank House
Black Prince Road
London SE1 7SJ

Tel. 071-582 7972
Fax 071-735 1555
Represents the interests of non-profit-maximising, community-based radio projects, and provides advice, information, training and consultancy for its members.

*CSV Media*
237 Pentonville Road
London N1 9NJ
Tel. 071-278 6601
A charity providing media training and assisting charities to devise broadcast campaigns.

*Independent Programme Producers' Association*
50-51 Berwick Street
London W1A 4RD
Tel. 071-439 7034
Fax 071-494 2700

*Independent Television Commission (ITC)*
70 Brompton Road
London SW3 1EY
Tel. 071-584 7011
Fax 071-589 5533
Publishes TV Take-up, which gives information on educational programmes for adults on ITV and Channel 4.

*Institute of Local Television*
13 Bellevue Place
Edinburgh
EH7 4BS
Tel. 031-557 8610

*International Broadcasting Trust*
2 Ferdinand Place
London NW1 8EE
Tel. 071-482 2847

A charity which produces programmes and educational material on international environmental and developmental issues. It also acts as a media pressure group arguing for more television air time to be devoted to third world issues.

*National Union of Journalists*
Acorn House
314-20 Grays Inn Road
London WC1X 8DP
Tel. 071-278 7916

*Press Complaints Commission*
1 Salisbury Square
London EC4Y 8AE
Tel. 071-353 1248
Fax 071-353 8355

*Press Council*
1 Salisbury Square
London EC4Y 8AE
Tel. 071-353 1248

*Shadow Radio Authority*
c/o ITC (above)

*Volunteer Centre*
29 Lower King's Road
Berkhamsted
Herts HP4 2AB
Tel. 04427-73311
The Media Project at the Volunteer Centre was set up in 1977 to help voluntary and statutory organisations make more effective use of the broadcasting media. Although the project ended in 1990, the Volunteer Centre still has archives which provide a good resource on volunteering and social action broadcasting. Liz Schofield can provide advice and information on volunteering linked to broadcasting.

# Organisations offering training courses in using the media

*Councils for voluntary service (CVS)*
A number - about a third - of CVS have run some kind of media training day or days for local voluntary organisations. It is worth enquiring whether your local CVS has run, or is going to run, such events, or, if not, suggest the possibility. You can get the address of your local CVS from libraries, town halls or the local telephone directory, or from the National Association of Councils for Voluntary Service on 0742-786636

*CTVC (Churches Television and Radio Centre)*
Hillside
Merry Hill Road
Bushey
Watford WD2 1DR
Tel. 081-950 4426/7
CTVC runs training courses in television and radio presentation and broadcasting techniques. Courses are run at reduced cost for members of charitable organisations. Enquiries should be made to the training co-ordinator.

*National Council for the Training of Journalists*
Carlton House
Hemnall Street
Epping
Essex CM16 4NL
Tel. 0378-72395
NCTJ runs a number of short courses for journalists including sub-editing, news editing and writing, which might be of interest to press officers wishing to improve their writing and editing skills. NCTJ also refers journalists to courses on broadcasting run by the Preston Polytechnic (tel. 0305-22141), Darlington College of Technology (tel. 0325-467651) and Highbury College, Portsmouth (tel. 0772-383131).

*Volunteer Centre UK*
29 Lower King's Road
Berkhamsted
Herts HP4 2AB
Tel. 0442-873311
Fax 0442-870852
The Volunteer Centre provides a range of training for people who work
with volunteers, including use of the media. People should address
enquiries to the training unit.


# Guides and directories

*Benn's Press Directory*
From:
Benn Business Information Services Ltd
Union House
Eridge Road
Tunbridge Wells
Kent TN4 8HF
Tel. 0892-38991
Published each year in November

*Brad UK Press Guide*
From:
BRAD
76 Oxford Street
London WIR 1RB
Tel. 071-434 2233
Issued monthly

*Mediadisk*
Software package listing approximately 8,000 journals to enable PR
companies and practitioners to produce press lists.
From:
PR Planner UK
Hale House
290-296 Green Lanes
London N13 5TP

Tel. 081-882 0155

*PIMS Media Directory*
From:
PIMS (London) Ltd
Faber Court
4 St John's Place
St John's Square
London EC1M 4AH
Tel. 071-250 0870

*PNA Targetter*
Lists over 11,000 journals on software.
From:
PNA
Communications House
210 Old Street
London EC1V 9UN
Tel. 071-490 8111

*PR Planner*
From:
Media Information Ltd
Hale House
290-296 Green Lanes
London N13 5TP
Tel. 081-882 9155

*Willings Press Guide*
From:
Thomas Skinner Directories
Windsor Court
East Grinstead House
East Grinstead
Sussex RH19 1XA
Tel. 0342-26972
Published annually

# Press-cutting agencies

*Durrants Press Cuttings Ltd*
11 Northburgh Street
London EC1V 0JL
Tel. 071-251 4918

*Romeike and Curtice*
Hale House
290-296 Green Lanes
London N13 5TP
Tel. 081-882-0155

# Press release and distribution services

*PNA Services Ltd*
13-19 Curtain Road
London EC2A 3LT
Tel. 071-377 2521

# Appendix 2
# Useful Publications

Anwar. *Ethnic Minority Broadcasting*, Commission for racial Equality, 1983.

Joanne Bornet. *Have You Heard?*, Help the Aged in association with the London Voluntary Services Council and Greater London Association for Pre-Retirement, 1981.

British Film Institute. *Film and Television Handbook*, BFI, published annually.

Dickinson. *How to Take on the Media*, Weidenfeld & Nicholson, 1990.

Jane Drinkwater. *Get It on Radio and Television*, Pluto Press, 1984. Available from London Media Project, 237 Pentonville Road, London N1 9NJ.

Heseltine. *Public Relations for Voluntary Youth Organisations*, National Council for Voluntary Youth Services, 1987.

Gemma Littlehails. *Upfront: A Public Relations Guide*, National Marriage Guidance Council, 1985.

Dorothy & Alastair McIntosh. *A Basic Public Relations Guide for Charities*, Directory of Social Change, 1985.

Richard Mills. *Media Choices*, Oxford University Press, 1990.

Sarah Morrison (chair of working party). *Broadcasting and Voluntary Action, Briefing Paper: Competition, Choice and Quality?*, Volunteer Centre UK, 1987.

Nicola Parker (ed). *Charities and Broadcasting: A Guide to Radio and Television Appeals and Grants*, Directory of Social Change, 1988.

Simon Partridge. *Not the BBC/IBA*, Comedia Minority Press Group Series No.8, 1982.

Porter. *User's Guide to the Media*, Inter-varsity, 1988.

David Saint. *Let's Get Publicity and Get It Right*, Printforce, 1989.

Sergeant & Jones. *Social Uses of Broadcasting*, Volunteer Centre UK, 1989.

Sue Ward. *Getting the Message Across: Public Relations, Publicity, and Working with the Media*, Journeyman, 1991.

Des Wilson. *Pressure: The A to Z of Campaigning in Britain*, Heinemann Educational Books Ltd, 1984.

# Appendix 3
# Press Complaints
# Commission

## Code of Practice

This is the new Code of Practice for journalists which will underpin the Press Complaints Commission, which replaces the Press Council.

It was drawn up by an industry working party chaired by Patsy Chapman, editor of the *News of the World*. They considered proposals put forward by the Calcutt Committee and also took account of the proposed Press Council Code and the existing Newspaper Publishers Association Code.

All members of the Press have a duty to maintain the highest professional and ethical standards. In doing so, they should have regard to the provisions of this code of practice and to safeguarding the public's right to know.

Editors are responsible for the actions of journalists employed by their publications. They should also satisfy themselves as far as possible that material accepted from non-staff members was obtained in accordance with this code.

While recognising that this involves a substantial element of self-restraint by editors and journalists, it is designed to be acceptable in the context of a system of self-regulation. The code applies in the spirit as well as in the letter.

# 1. ACCURACY

(i)  Newspapers and periodicals should take care not to publish inaccurate, misleading or distorted material.

(ii)  Whenever it is recognised that a significant inaccuracy, misleading statement or distorted report has been published, it should be corrected promptly and with due prominence.

(iii)  An apology should be published whenever appropriate.

(iv)  A newspaper or periodical should always report fairly and accurately the outcome of an action for defamation to which it has been a party.

# 2. OPPORTUNITY TO REPLY

A fair opportunity for reply to inaccuracies should be given to individuals or organisations when reasonably called for.

# 3. COMMENT, CONJECTURE AND FACT

Newspapers, while free to be partisan, should distinguish clearly between comment, conjecture and fact.

# 4. PRIVACY

Intrusions and enquiries into an individual's private life without his or her consent are not generally acceptable and publication can only be justified when in the public interest. This would include:

(i)  Detecting or exposing crime or serious misdemeanour.

(ii)  Detecting or exposing seriously anti-social conduct.

(iii)  Protecting public health and safety.

(iv)  Preventing the public from being misled by some statement or action of that individual.

# 5. HOSPITALS

(i)  Journalists or photographers making enquiries at hospitals or similar institutions should identify themselves to a responsible official and obtain permission before entering non-public areas.

(ii)  The restrictions on intruding into privacy are particularly relevant to enquiries about individuals in hospital or similar institutions.

## 6. MISREPRESENTATION

(i)   Journalists should not generally obtain or seek to obtain information or pictures through misrepresentation or subterfuge.

(ii)  Unless in the public interest, documents or photographs should be removed only with the express consent of the owner.

(iii) Subterfuge can be justified only in the public interest and only when material cannot be obtained by any other means.
      In all these clauses the public interest includes:

- Detecting or exposing crime or serious misdemeanour.
- Detecting or exposing anti-social conduct.
- Protecting public health or safety.
- Preventing the public being misled by some statement or action of an individual or organisation.

## 7. HARASSMENT

(i)   Journalists should neither obtain information or pictures through intimidation or harassment.

(ii)  Unless their enquiries are in the public interest, journalists should not photograph individuals on private property without their consent: should not persist in telephoning or questioning individuals after having been asked to desist: should not remain on their property after having been asked to leave and should not follow them.

The public interest would include:

- detecting or exposing crime or serious misdemeanour;
- detecting or exposing anti-social conduct;
- protecting public health and safety;
- preventing the public from being misled by some statement or action of that individual organisation.

## 8. PAYMENT FOR ARTICLES

(i)   Payments or offers of payment for stories, pictures or information should not be made to witnesses or potential witnesses in current criminal proceedings or to people engaged

in crime or to their associates except where the material concerned ought to be published in the public interest and the payment is necessary for this to be done.
The public interest will include:

- detecting or exposing crime or serious misdemeanour;
- detecting or exposing anti-social conduct;
- protecting public health and safety;
- preventing the public from being misled by some statement or action of that individual organisation.

(ii) 'Associates' includes family, friends, neighbours and colleagues.
(iii) Payments should not be made either directly or indirectly through agents.

## 9. INTRUSION INTO GRIEF OR SHOCK
In cases involving personal grief or shock, enquiries should be carried out and approaches made with sympathy and discretion.

## 10. INNOCENT RELATIVES AND FRIENDS
The Press should generally avoid identifying relatives or friends of persons convicted or accused of crime unless the reference to them is necessary for the full, fair and accurate reporting of the crime or legal proceedings.

## 11. INTERVIEWING OR PHOTOGRAPHING CHILDREN

(i) Journalists should not normally interview or photograph children under the age of 16 on subjects involving the personal welfare of the child, in the absence or without the consent of a parent or other adult who is responsible for the children.

(ii) Children should not be approached or photographed while at school without the permission of the school authorities.

## 12. CHILDREN IN SEX CASES
The Press should not, even where the law does not prohibit it, identify children under the age of 16 who are involved in cases concerning sexual offences, whether as victims or as witnesses or defendants.

## 13. VICTIMS OF CRIME

The Press should not identify victims of sexual assault or publish material likely to contribute to such identification unless, by law, they are free to do so.

## 14. DISCRIMINATION

(i)  The Press should avoid prejudicial or pejorative reference to a person's race, colour, religion, sex or sexual orientation or to any physical or mental illness or handicap.

(ii)  It should avoid publishing details of a person's race, colour, religion, sex or sexual orientation, unless these are directly relevant to the story.

## 15. FINANCIAL JOURNALISM

(i)  Even where the law does not prohibit it, journalists should not use for their own profit financial information they receive in advance of its general publication, or should they pass such information to others.

(ii)  They should not write about share or securities in whose performance they know that they or their close families have a significant financial interest, without disclosing the interest to the editor or financial editor.

(iii)  They should not buy or sell, either directly or through nominees or agents, shares or securities about which they have written recently or about which they intend to write in the near future.

## 16. CONFIDENTIAL SOURCES

Journalists have a moral obligation to protect confidential sources of information.

Source: *UK Press Gazette* (10 December 1990)

# Index

# The Voluntary Agencies Directory 1991

## The Social Activists' Bible

NCVO's directory of voluntary agencies is the standard reference work for anyone who cares about helping the community. It lists nearly 2,000 leading voluntary agencies, ranging from small, specialist self-help groups to long-established national charities. It gives concise, up-to-date descriptions of their aims and activities with details of

| | |
|---|---|
| charitable status | local branches |
| volunteer participation | membership |
| trading activities | staffing |

A list of useful addresses includes professional and public advisory bodies concerned with voluntary action; a classified index and quick reference list of acronyms and abbreviations give easy access to entries.

There is extensive coverage of groups concerned with women's issues, minority rights, self-help, community development and leisure activities, environment and conservation, campaigning and consumer affairs.

Voluntary agencies play an important part in making the world a better place to live in. This NCVO directory is the essential guide to their work.

'If you buy only one directory of voluntary agencies, buy this one and buy it every year.'            *Health Libraries Review*

'...an essential working tool.'                    *Environment Now*

**£10.95**

# The Women's Directory
## Compiled by Fiona Macdonald

*The Women's Directory* will enable women who wish to make contact with others - whether for social, cultural, sporting, charitable, self-help or political purposes - to locate and identify suitable groups and organisations. It refers women to appropriate 'umbrella' bodies, whether voluntary, local-government based or state funded, and gives other sources of information about women's activities, including relevant magazines and journals, publishers and bookshops. Information is presented in an accessible, simple-to-follow format, with symbols used to give additional information.

£6.95

# BSP Practical Guides

Titles in the series:

All books are available through bookshops and can be purchased from NCVO Reception during office hours.  In case of difficulty books can be ordered by post direct from Plymbridge Distributors Ltd, Estover Road, Plymouth PL6 7PZ (tel. 0752-705251) adding 12½% to total value of order for post and packing (minimum 45p).